T0305118

Cost–Benefit Analysis and Distributional Preferences

Cost–Benefit Analysis and Distributional Preferences

A Choice Modelling Approach

Helen Scarborough
Senior Lecturer
School of Accounting, Economics and Finance
Deakin University, Warrnambool, Australia

Jeff Bennett
Professor of Environmental Management,
Crawford School of Economics and Government
The Australian National University, Canberra, Australia

Edward Elgar
Cheltenham, UK • Northampton, MA, USA

Published by
Edward Elgar Publishing Limited
The Lypiatts
15 Lansdown Road
Cheltenham
Glos GL50 2JA
UK

Edward Elgar Publishing, Inc.
William Pratt House
9 Dewey Court
Northampton
Massachusetts 01060
USA

A catalogue record for this book
is available from the British Library

Library of Congress Control Number 2011939350

ISBN 978 0 85793 222 8

Printed and bound by MPG Books Group, UK

Contents

Tables

Figures

Acknowledgements

We are grateful to a number of colleagues who have provided valuable input and discussion as the development of the ideas in this book has progressed; particularly, Prof. Michael Burton from The University of Western Australia, and Prof. Graeme Wines and Dr Rodney Carr from Deakin University. We would also like to thank Prof. Alan Randall for his support, thoughtful review and gracious Foreword. The book would not have been completed without the efficient and thorough editing of Dr Chris Ulyatt: thank you, Chris, for your professional approach and good humour. And finally, thanks to Ngaire and Bob for their support.

Helen Scarborough and Jeff Bennett

Foreword

The times are ripe for some serious grappling with issues of distributional equity. Harsh austerity measures are being imposed on ordinary people in resource-poor countries on the periphery of Europe at the behest of the overpaid international bankers who caused the global financial crisis in the first place. In the US, the Tea Party movement, fragmented as it is, includes billionaires who fund disaffected ordinary people to demand public sector frugality that would surely make their own lots in life more difficult. All of this is happening at a time when the distribution of income and wealth in the more prosperous countries is wider than it has been for a century.

A growing sense of global limits under pressure is colliding with the customary optimism that future generations will have things better than their predecessors, and ordinary citizens are responding with everything from green politics to 'shoot the messenger' climate scepticism.

So, what better time for a book demonstrating that familiar methods of non-market valuation can be adapted readily for learning about the preferences of ordinary people regarding intergenerational distribution? Helen Scarborough and Jeff Bennett have produced a work that is genuinely path-breaking. As is often the case with path-breaking work, the idea is simple enough: if people can respond to choice experiments in ways that tell us a lot about what they value and how much they value it, why would they not be able to respond to choice experiments where the options offered have different distributional consequences? Such simple ideas evade implementation not because they are so hard to think up, but because it is so easy to dismiss them as unthinkable. All credit goes to Scarborough and Bennett for busting through this particular unthinkability barrier.

The authors demonstrate the use of choice modelling (CM) in the particular context of intergenerational distribution, covering all aspects from survey design to the analysis of results carefully and in considerable detail. This thorough treatment is valuable in its own right, and will serve as a model for future applications of CM, many of them on quite different topics.

Scarborough and Bennett bite off a lot more than choice experiments with a distributional dimension. They blast through the idea of distributional preferences to grapple with equity, a much more complicated concept. Their experiments address intergenerational distribution, which brings its own special problems in addition to all the problems raised by distribution and equity per se. They frame their empirical results first in terms of intergenerational welfare weights for use in cost–benefit analysis, and later as downward adjustment factors for social discount rates. Considering the complications thus introduced, and the massive literature from economics and beyond addressing most of these topics, it must surely have occurred to Scarborough and Bennett that they were tilting at some windmills and flirting with some of the third rails in economics and moral philosophy.

Let me offer a few hints of the complexities their work raises.

What constitutes *equity* is by no means obvious. Possibilities include that people receive what they deserve, people have equal opportunity to pursue happiness, people have a secure safety-net ensuring that their basic needs can be met, and society values equality of outcome so highly that it measures social welfare as the welfare of the worst-off member.

The standard view of the *cost–benefit (CB) criterion* is that it identifies proposed projects and policies that would increase the size of the game. These projects and policies usually offer goods and services of various kinds, and it is a standard result in economics that it is cheaper (equally cheap at worst) to achieve a given utility gain by giving the beneficiary money than by giving cheese (unless, of course, the government already has stockpiled lots of cheese to remove 'excess' supply from the market). With that in mind, one needs to be deeply pessimistic about the state of society's redistributive institutions, in order to propose a weighted-CB criterion that would systematically approve projects that reduce the size of the game in order to deliver benefits to favoured groups.

Intergenerational distribution issues get really complicated when there is overlap among the generations concerned. Understanding the implications of redistribution toward distant future generations is difficult enough, but the case of redistribution among overlapping generations that can and do make all manner of intergenerational accommodations ramps up the challenge dramatically. Governments seeking to help the very young usually settle for subsidizing their parents, and for good reasons. The middle-aged support retirement programmes and the elderly support favourable tax treatment of inheritances, when the opposite pattern of support is equally plausible, because there is a good deal of convergence between middle-aged and elderly interests in these cases. This makes it hard to interpret an experimental finding that, say, ordinary people favour redistribution toward the very young – are they telling us they want to help those not yet capable of providing for themselves, or that they want people who will be middle-aged 50 years from now to be better off than today's 50-year-olds?

In recent years, there has been a spate of novel suggestions for re-jigging the *social discount rate* to promote intergenerational equity – clearly this is not a settled issue. To the extent that social discount rates include positive time preference – that is, assume a degree of myopia – it might be argued they should be reduced systematically in response to intergenerational equity arguments. Even if that much is granted, questions remain open as to whether such equity issues are resolved by the preferences of ordinary people, revealed in an overlapping-generations context.

The value of the Scarborough–Bennett contribution does not hinge on whether it resolves, in a single brief book, all of these issues convincingly. It has earned its place on the bookshelf as a successful proof-of-concept exercise, demonstrating that ordinary citizens can grapple coherently with choices involving overt distributional elements. The list of potential applications of that insight seems very long. The value of knowing how people feel about distribution does not depend on resolution of the controversies that have bedevilled classical welfare economics since its beginning.

The impact of a book is the outcome of a complex interaction between the authors, the text, and the readers, which suggests that the research agenda potentially arising from this work is much richer than the authors have announced, and may well exceed their most optimistic anticipations. With publication, authors lose control as their ideas enter the public domain and grow and develop in ways they did not anticipate. Helen Scarborough and Jeff Bennett may be surprised by the magnitude and the nature of the impact this work eventually enjoys.

Alan Randall

The University of Sydney
and
The Ohio State University

1. Distribution and environmental policy

1.0 INTRODUCTION

The question of a 'fair' allocation is one with which we all grapple in many contexts. For those in decision-making positions such as policy-makers, teachers and parents, it involves the difficult task of weighing up competing claims. These claims may be presented on the basis of allowing for special needs, compensating for handicaps, rewarding additional effort or striving for equality. Economists are well aware that, as a society, we are not able to meet the unlimited wants of each individual. The fundamental issue of scarcity necessitates decisions about allocation. The questions of how resources are used as efficiently as possible to maximize the well-being of people and how the distribution of resources is made 'equitably' are fundamental questions in economics. This book focuses on the latter question – that is, the equity or distributional aspect of economic analysis.

The complexity of the notion of social justice confounds research into the equity principles and preferences held by the community. As will be discussed in Chapter 2, it is assumed that each individual has distributional preferences which can be interpreted in a social welfare ordering. Social welfare preferences may be based on a variety of justice principles. General ethical principles underlying discussions about fair allocation fall into several categories. The principles either formulate more specific interpretations of utilitarianism, where the well-being of each individual is summed, or apply alternative or complementary ethical frameworks (Banuri et al. 1996). For example, distributional preferences may be based on rewards according to contribution, equality of opportunity or equality of outcome. Konow (2001) categorizes three basic principles of justice: accountability, efficiency and needs. Accountability calls for allocations to be in proportion to volitional contributions, efficiency encompasses the provision of incentives for productivity and needs for allocations to be sufficient to meet each individual's basic requirements for life.

In many instances, the relative importance of these justice principles is related to issues of context. The area of policy analysis influences the weighing up of different justice principles. Furthermore, within different policy contexts the major distributional issues are likely to vary. For example, if the emphasis is on educational policy, the distributional issues to be considered may be the balance of resources between the public and private sectors or between the primary, secondary and tertiary sectors.

This book adopts a relatively narrow focus on the question of incorporating equity in policy analysis and concentrates on distribution within the context of natural resource management and environmental policy. This is one policy area where there is a growing awareness of the need for equity considerations to be an integral aspect of analysis and where information on distributional preferences would be valuable to decision-makers (Bennett 2003). Although our focus is primarily on the area of natural resource management and environmental policy, the methodological advances are relevant and applicable to other areas of policy development.

1.1 DISTRIBUTION AND ENVIRONMENTAL POLICY

Two fundamental principles underlie environmental policy decisions: efficiency in the allocation of resources and analysis of their distributional impacts. Economists are generally more confident in dealing with the former than with the latter. Yet, resource management policies have a range of distributional effects within the economy. It is unlikely that those benefiting from a specific policy change will be the same group as those who bear the cost. The environmental justice movement, both in principle and in terms of practical political action, emphasizes the distributional implications of environmental change (Agyeman et al. 2003). Tietenberg (2006, p. 503) argues that paying attention to environmental justice is desirable for two reasons:

> The ethical dimension concerns whether the distribution of risks, benefits and costs is in accordance with the norms of social justice. The desire for just policies is a conventional complement to the desire for efficient policies. The pragmatic dimension emphasizes the relationship between the distributional burden and both the likelihood that environmental legislation will pass and its ultimate form.

Assessment of the distributional impacts of environmental policy alternatives can be based on criteria such as the economic status, ethnicity, age, geographical or temporal distribution of those who gain and those who lose. As awareness of the distributional impacts of environmental policy change has heightened, debates have increasingly involved these distributional considerations (Serret and Johnstone 2006). For example, the geographic distribution of the gains and costs of environmental policy between regions, nations and countries is discussed in the literature, particularly with respect to climate change (see, for example, Fankhauser et al. 1997; Rose et al. 1998; Lange 2006). Even though environmental policies may be in everyone's joint interest, any individual, government or organization has an incentive to free-ride on others' contributions and spend their potential contributions on social and environmental problems in their own countries or regions. Hence, a dollar of benefit or cost may not be considered equally depending on the location of the recipient of the benefit or bearer of the cost.

Another prominent distributional issue in an environmental context is the income or wealth levels of those bearing costs or receiving gains. The aim is not to achieve a particular income distribution through environmental policy. It is more appropriate for that objective to be the target of the tax system and fiscal policy. Nevertheless, environmental policies affect various income groups and it is useful to consider whether respondents view costs and benefits differently depending on the financial standing of those involved. Some researchers have reported that the environmental and social benefits of growth have accrued to richer groups while the costs have fallen mainly on the poor (Adelman and Morris 1973; Ahluwalia 1975; Islam et al. 2003). Pearce (2006, p. 60) concludes that the evidence is 'probably leaning towards the view that existing environmental quality and income are negatively correlated in many cases'.

The issues of property rights and the sharing of the cost burden of policy are also prominent within the literature on the distributional issues of natural resource management and environmental policy. It is possible that respondents' notions of distributional justice are influenced by whether they believe the recipient has a right to a particular benefit or is responsible for the cost. This is supported by the social justice literature. Bojer (2003) argues that one of the factors that creates inequality is the ownership of natural resources and that it is often difficult to regard these inequalities as merited. For example, Atkinson et al. (2000) used a contingent ranking study to elicit preferences of the population with respect to sharing the burden of the cost of environmental policy. Using the characteristics of the groups between whom the cost burden could be shared as 'those responsible, those likely to benefit and those with ability to pay', they found that the notion of property rights influences respondents' views regarding distributional justice. One difficulty with this approach is that these groups are not necessarily mutually exclusive.

The question of distribution is further complicated because distributional preferences may be asymmetrical and allocating positives may not be viewed in the same vein as the sharing of the burden of negatives. In the area of environmental policy, the sharing of the burden of costs is sometimes the politically more crucial issue compared with the allocation of benefits. Hence, when assessing natural resource policy options, the major challenges facing policy-makers and the community lie not only with assessing the extent of the benefits and costs of policy alternatives but also in determining the distributional impacts of environmental options. Who will benefit and who will be disadvantaged? How do we determine if distributional changes are 'acceptable'? As Kristöm (2006, p. 129) asserts, while environmental economists have been focusing on efficiency issues, the fact that equity is important in shaping environmental policy is increasingly being appreciated. There is a growing awareness that a priority in the process of shaping environmental policy should be to evaluate its distributional impacts comprehensively. In order to assess the full impact of an environmental policy decision, it is necessary to consider the distributional impacts resulting from policy options as well as their efficiency consequences.

The desirability of such a comprehensive approach to environmental policy analysis has been widely recognized. For example, the United Nations Programme of Action resulting from the 1992 Rio Earth Summit (UNCED 1993, p. 66) called for improved decision-making processes as part of the declaration on environment and development.

> Governments should …, improve the processes of decision-making so as to achieve the progressive integration of economic, social and environmental issues in the pursuit of development that is economically efficient, socially equitable and responsible and environmentally sound.

While there is much discussion about this economic, social and environmental 'triple bottom line', the integration of equity in policy analysis is complex and far from resolved.

1.2 INCORPORATING DISTRIBUTION IN COST–BENEFIT ANALYSIS

In terms of economic approaches to decision-making, one of the most widely accepted methods of assessing various policy options is the application of cost–benefit analysis (CBA) (Farrow and Toman 1998). With rigorous foundations in the theory of welfare economics, a CBA approach suggests that a project is deemed worthwhile if the benefits it creates for society outweigh its costs. However, a challenge associated with applying CBA as a decision-making tool is the means of incorporating the distributional impacts of policy changes in the decision-making calculus. While knowledge of who bears the costs and who reaps the benefits of resource management decisions is often available, the analysis of such distributional implications of decisions is limited, despite their importance (Dorfman 1977; Markandya 1998).

The conceptual structure of CBA provides for the incorporation of distributional considerations, along with efficiency impacts, into the decision-making process through the use of *distributional weights*. For example, if benefits are being enjoyed by a poorer or disadvantaged group, these benefits can receive a higher weighting in a CBA assessment.

This book addresses this issue of incorporating distributional weights in CBA. It draws on the extensive body of theory in welfare economics to focus on the application of distributional weights in CBA. The application of distributional weights facilitates the incorporation of distributional analysis into CBA assessments of environmental policy options. But the option of including distributional weights in CBA is contentious. As discussed in more detail in Chapter 2, there has been considerable debate within the economics literature about the appropriateness of weighting costs and benefits when using CBA to evaluate policy changes. And despite being conceptually possible, there has been reluctance amongst policy-makers to adopt the approach.

A review of the literature suggests a number of reasons for this reluctance. There is debate about whether incorporating distribution is within the role of economic analysis, due to the value judgements involved. Even if it is accepted that weights should be applied, there is complexity in determining how to estimate the weights and whose distributional preferences should be reflected in the weights. Furthermore, determining what factors contributing to utility should be included in the weighting process is problematic. Consequently, despite strong theoretical foundations, the application of distributional weights in policy analysis is not common practice.

While economists are unresolved in their approach to this issue, in practice, policy-makers are left with two options: applying no distributional weights or applying *implicit* weights. If no weights are applied, each one dollar of benefits and costs is treated equally, regardless of who bears the cost or reaps the benefit. In effect, the assumption being applied is that the marginal social value of income, or additional consumption, is equal for all individuals. This assumption has two aspects: first, that an extra one dollar of benefit or cost will impact equally on the well-being of each group within the community and, second, that the well-being of all groups within the community is treated equally in each individual's assessment of social welfare. The problem is that these assumptions are unrealistic and, in essence, ignoring distributional concerns still implies the application of a particular set of weights. Alternatively, if implicit weights are imposed, it is the distributional preferences of the policy-maker that are being applied.

In part, this is due to difficulties in the determination of objective weights. The issue is whether it is possible to elicit the social welfare preferences of the community and estimate distributional weights suitable for application in CBA. One method which has been applied to explore distributional preferences is game theory experiments (see, for example, Güth and van Damme 1998; Selten and Ockenfels 1998; Bolton and Ockenfels 2000). The results of these experiments provide insight into the social justice principles applied by respondents in determining allocations. For example, although egalitarian principles are often assumed, these studies indicate that in a variety of different scenarios, when faced with choices which result in different pay-offs, people are willing to sacrifice little to defend egalitarian distributional preferences where equal pay-offs for each participant result.

This book explores a further potential method for addressing the limited knowledge of the distributional preferences of the community; that is, the application of the stated preference method of choice modelling to the estimation of distributional preferences.

1.3 CHOICE MODELLING AND DISTRIBUTIONAL WEIGHTS

Choice modelling is a stated preference method that has been widely used in transport and marketing economics and, more recently, in environmental economics. Stated choice methods encompass a range of stated preference techniques which take a similar approach to estimating values for changes in non-market goods. The origins of choice modelling are in conjoint analysis (derived from the two words 'considered jointly') and contingent valuation methods in the environmental and health literatures. The method has evolved through advances in a variety of disciplines where the 'common goal has been the development of methods to explain individual and aggregate choice behaviour' (Louviere et al. 2000).

Generally, the focus of choice modelling research in an environmental context has been to estimate values for non-market environmental goods and services. Stated preference techniques such as choice modelling rely on eliciting consumer preferences through some form of questionnaire approach. In conventional applications, the aim is to identify the utility that individuals have for the attributes of goods or services by examining the trade-offs implicit in choices. This provides the flexibility to predict behavioural responses to changing opportunities. By varying the levels of the scenario attributes, it is possible to understand respondents' preferences and gain insight into the trade-offs that respondents make between attributes. This allows the estimation of a variety of opportunity costs and willingness to pay. One of the strengths of this methodology is that it forces respondents to consider substitution possibilities. Hence the method is useful not only as a value estimation technique but also for assessing policy options. This may involve presenting respondents with a description of alternative policy options and seeking an indication of the single preferred option.

In conventional applications, choice modelling provides two different types of value estimates. The first, known as implicit prices, are estimates of the value of a change in an environmental or social attribute. These are based on the marginal rate of substitution between a cost or dollar value attribute and a non-monetary attribute. The second type of value estimates are compensating surpluses, which show respondents' willingness to pay for a bundle of changes. This may be different from the sum of the changes in the implicit prices if the value that respondents have for a bundle of changes is not simply the sum of the value of the individual changes. A significant advantage of the choice modelling approach is that it is possible to estimate the willingness of the respondent to pay for more of an environmental attribute.

This book focuses on the application of choice modelling to the estimation of distributional preferences. In this instance it is assumed that respondents are maximizing their social welfare preferences rather than their individual utility preferences. Choice modelling provides the opportunity for respondents to express their stated preferences, in this case their social welfare preferences; that is, how they believe resources and goods and services should be allocated between groups within the community. A strength of the method is that respondents are continually forced to weigh up competing claims, which is a fundamental aspect of incorporating equity in policy analysis. A further advantage with the application of choice modelling to the estimation of distributional preferences is the ability to estimate the equity preferences of the community, thereby enabling policy-makers to gain enhanced understanding of community preferences.

In order to demonstrate the application of choice modelling to the estimation of distributional weights, a choice modelling application case study is reported in Chapters 4 and 5. The case study centres on one specific distributional question: the distribution of goods and services between generations. The case study provides the background for the subsequent discussion of the opportunities and challenges of using this stated preference method to estimate distributional preferences. The debate about the incorporation of distributional preferences in CBA is also advanced by demonstrating the application of the stated preference method of choice modelling to the estimation of equity preferences and a set of distributional weights suitable for application in a CBA setting.

1.4 CASE STUDY: DISTRIBUTION BETWEEN GENERATIONS

With growing public awareness of the impact of environmental decisions on future generations, the question of the distributional preferences of the current generation with respect to intergenerational equity is an integral aspect of environmental policy decision-making. This is often presented under the banner of sustainability, with much of the sustainability literature emphasizing the goal of intergenerational equity. This reinforces the importance of the clarification of what is meant by the term intergenerational equity.

Some of the literature supports the conjecture that the community has positive preferences towards future generations. Arrow et al. (2004) suggest that distributional preferences may favour future generations and explain this inference by contending that individuals 'derive a positive externality, outside of the marketplace, from the welfare of future generations'. Similarly, Arrow and Kurz (1970) suggest that each individual derives satisfaction from having wealth added to future generations. In part this may be construed as altruism which reflects interdependent utility functions and is theoretically distinct from the social welfare approach adopted here and outlined in Chapter 2.

Nevertheless, the literature on altruism provides insight into understanding intergenerational distributional preferences and suggests positive preferences toward future generations. Using data from a *Washington Post* survey, Popp (2001) found evidence of what he defines as weak altruism, where neither strong altruism nor pure self-interest holds toward future generations. Altruistic motives toward environmental protection for the benefit of future generations may also influence non-use values (Popp 2001). Non-use values which influence the utility of future generations include:[1]

- option values – values associated with knowing that a resource is available for possible use in the future;
- existence values – values associated with simply knowing that a resource exists;[2] and
- bequest values – the value of passing environmental resources on to future generations.

Literature in other fields of economics also provides some insights into the question of intergenerational preferences. Within the area of health economics, cost-effectiveness analysis usually assumes that a quality-adjusted life-year is of equal value to everybody. However, Rodríguez and Pinto (2000, p. 619) discuss the possibility of weighting health benefits for age and present results of an experiment which found that 'in the sample studied, the social value of equivalent health gains was considered to be different for people of different ages'. Their findings supported the premise of additional weighting being applied to benefits accruing to younger people.

Intergenerational distribution is also relevant within the area of public finance with respect to the timing of government taxation and spending commitments leading to transfers between generations, particularly due to superannuation liabilities. In Australia, concern for the possible debt burden to be inherited by future generations resulted in the establishment of a 'Future Fund' and an emphasis on a 'sustainable fiscal policy framework', as indicated in the Intergenerational Reports published by the Australian Government (Commonwealth of Australia 2007, 2010).

Although much of the literature suggests positive preferences toward future generations, there is also evidence to support the opposing view. There are two main counter arguments. The first is that future generations do not require special treatment because they are likely to be better off than the current generation, given that they are likely to inherit enhanced stocks of capital and knowledge

(Turner 1988). This argument is also discussed by Gollier (2002a, p. 464) who suggests that 'with a sure positive growth of the economy, we do not want to benefit overmuch future generations who will enjoy a larger GNP per capita'.

The second argument is that economics is premised on the foundation that individuals are self-interested. With this in mind, it is assumed that the rational behaviour for each individual is to maximize the utility of the generation to which they belong. It may be argued that the extent of environmental degradation illustrates little concern by the current generation for the utility of future generations. This suggests a disparity between the rhetoric of the literature and the practical reality.

The results of the case study reported in Chapter 5 contribute to this debate by presenting quantifiable intergenerational distributional weights which suggest positive preferences towards future generations. As discussed at the end of the chapter, these findings have significant policy implications. One particularly interesting aspect of the policy implications which is explored is the link between the application of intergenerational distributional weights and the social discount rate (Scarborough 2011).

1.5 THE STRUCTURE OF THE BOOK

This book is structured as follows. Chapter 2 introduces the welfare economic theory from which CBA has evolved. It addresses the theory underpinning the derivation of distributional weights and provides an overview of the history of the debate within the economics literature about the validity of applying distributional weights in CBA. The manner in which distributional weights reflect social justice preferences is also outlined. The general questions to be discussed – whether distributional weights are equal to one and whether there is an alternative method for estimating distribution weights – are developed in this chapter.

The research method of choice modelling is introduced in Chapter 3. As indicated, in conventional applications, choice modelling is based on an assumption of utility maximization by respondents. This theory has been adapted and a random welfare model designed to estimate a social welfare function and, hence, social welfare preferences. The relationship between the output of the random welfare model and the distributional weights introduced in Chapter 2 concludes the chapter.

Chapter 4 details the development of the intergenerational distribution choice modelling application that has been conducted. In particular, there were a number of complex design issues involved in determining the alternatives, attributes and attribute levels for the choice model. Although presented in the context of the case study, these issues are relevant for the general development of the application of stated preference techniques to the estimation of distributional preferences. Chapter 5 presents data analysis and results for both the multi-nomial logit and mixed logit estimations of the intergenerational distribution choice data. The findings with respect to intergenerational equity preferences are discussed in the context of current natural resource and environmental policy.

The results of the case study promote many areas of discussion and these are the focus of Chapter 6. The research illustrates that the estimation of distribu-tional weights is possible; however, the subsequent discussion of the validity of the application of distributional weights remains contentious. There are challenges and opportunities associated with the application of choice model-ling to the estimation of distributional preferences and these are outlined in some detail. In part, this discussion highlights the need for further research in the areas of both distributional weighting in CBA and intergenerational equity specifically. Discussion of some of these challenging areas of potential research concludes Chapter 6.

The main objective of this book is to enhance the potential of CBA as a tool for decision-making. The incorporation of equity concerns in a comprehensive and theoretically rigorous manner is demonstrated by using choice modelling to estimate a set of distributional weights suitable for inclusion in a CBA setting. The estimation of distributional weights provides the potential for the inclusion of equity considerations in environmental policy decision-making.

It generally remains the role of economists to provide analysis and infor-mation relevant to choices relating to natural resource management, while those implementing policy make final decisions regarding environmental policy. This book aims to enhance the information available to policy-makers by promoting the theoretical framework for integrating the social dimension of environmental change into policy analysis.

NOTES

1. Weisbrod (1964) and Krutilla (1967) introduced the notion that economic value may accrue to individuals who do not actually 'use' environmental assets.
2. An early discussion of existence value is presented by Krutilla (1967). A more recent summary is provided in Brown and Shogren (2005).

2. Distributional weighting and cost–benefit analysis

2.0 INTRODUCTION

The conceptual foundations of the application of distributional weights in a CBA setting are well established in welfare economics theory. An understanding of the derivation of distributional weights is essential before one can proceed to their application in CBA and the incorporation of distributional preferences in policy analysis.

2.1 THE SOCIAL WELFARE UNDERPINNINGS OF COST–BENEFIT ANALYSIS

In decision-making between policy options, welfare economics provides a framework for understanding a social ordering over alternative possible states of the world (Boadway and Bruce 1984). It is based on three value judgements (Maler 1985):

- Each individual is the best judge of his/her own welfare.[1]
- The welfare of society depends on the individual welfare of its citizens.[2]
- If the welfare of one individual increases and the welfare of no-one decreases, the welfare of society increases. This is known as a Pareto improvement.

The problem in terms of policy analysis is one of ranking different resource allocations to maximize social welfare. Well-established theory indicates that in a two-person economy, a competitive market will exhaust all of the gains from trade and an equilibrium allocation will be achieved that is Pareto optimal; that is, an equilibrium where no one person can be made better off without someone else being made worse off. However, this market outcome, known as the *First Welfare Theorem*, does not address the question (amongst others) of the distribution of utility between individuals and groups within society. Although it provides insight into the efficiency of an outcome, the distributional impact of the outcome is undetermined. As the outcome depends on the original distribution of endowments, if this is changed a new equilibrium and a new Pareto optimum is reached.

Hence, one of the fundamental problems faced in assessing policy options is the comparison of welfare levels within the community. The competitive market provides a number of efficient outcomes that are Pareto optimal, but it does not provide a solution to the question of choosing between Pareto-optimal allocations. The Pareto criterion is inadequate as a basis for policy choice where gains to some groups and losses to others require comparison. Pareto optimality does not embody a concept of 'justice', and inequitable allocations may be optimal under the criterion. The underlying failing is that the Pareto criterion avoids making interpersonal comparisons, yet it is these comparisons that are required in most allocation decisions (Myles 1995).

2.1.1 Social Welfare Functions

The theory behind distributional weighting is based on the notion of a social welfare function (SWF), defined as an ordering of the set of alternative social states (Bergson 1938; Samuelson 1947). Technically, a social welfare ordering ranks social states or projects in terms of their impact on the welfare of the population. If the social welfare ordering is continuous, it can be translated into an SWF. Randall (1987) describes the SWF as a mathematical relationship precisely expressing the societal preferences about how economic well-being should be distributed among the individual members of society. The welfare function, W, can be written as:

$$W = w(z_1, z_2, \ldots z_n) \tag{2.1}$$

where W, which is usually considered to be ordinal, is a real valued function of all variables, (z_i), that might affect social welfare (Mueller 1989). The z_is and W are chosen to represent the ethical values of the society, or of the individuals in it (Samuelson 1947). While in theory a broad range of factors affect social welfare, economists have tended to concentrate on individual utility functions as a measure of social welfare.[3]

Therefore the SWF, W, is a function of utility U_i, for individuals, $i = 1, \ldots n$ in society.[4]

$$W = w(U_1, U_2, \ldots U_n) \tag{2.2}$$

In general, it is impossible to say whether or not a project having a positive present value improves welfare in society unless we know the properties of the SWF. An SWF is generally assumed to:

- Satisfy welfarism, which means that social welfare depends only on the utility of individuals.
- Be increasing with each individual's utility level and therefore satisfy the Pareto criterion.
- Display an intensity of trade-off between individuals' utilities that depends on the degree of inequality in society.
- Be indifferent about who enjoys a high or low level of utility. This principle is known as anonymity. Rawls (1971) developed an argument as to why society can agree in principle on a priori rules through the use of a hypothetical 'veil of ignorance'. It infers that individuals, from behind a veil of ignorance that screens knowledge of their future positions, unanimously agree on a redistribution formula (Johansson 1993).[5]

The most common form of the SWF is the utilitarian, where the utilities of individuals, $i...n$, are summed and the aim is to maximize the sum of the utilities, that is:

$$W(U_1 ... U_n) = \sum_{i=1}^{n} U_1 \qquad (2.3)$$

This is known as the classical utilitarian or Benthamite welfare function, developed by Bentham (1789) and championed by economists such as Mill (1863), Edgeworth (1881), Marshall (1890) and Pigou (1920). Utilitarianism has been, in many ways, the 'official' theory of traditional welfare economics (Sen 2000). There are, however, two particular limitations of utilitarianism as a theory of social welfare which are relevant. First, the process of aggregation can lead to an inability to distinguish between any two distributions that yield the same total utility. Hence, it can answer the efficiency question but not the equity question. Second, the assumption is conventionally made that each individual gets the same utility from the same commodity basket and, by adaptation, the same level of income (Sen 2000).[6] The commodity basket is assumed to be broad and include a range of goods and services such as health, education and the environment (Stern 2007).

The maximization of an SWF is invariably adopted as the objective of policy in public economics (Myles 1995). Importantly, the SWF emphasizes that society is concerned with the distribution of utility rather than the distribution of income. Each SWF represents one person's view of the allocation of utility across individuals in society. The focus of this book is to discuss the potential of non-market valuation techniques to elicit the distributional preferences of the general community as illustrated in each individual's SWF.

2.1.2 Properties of the SWF

The welfare economics originated by Pigou (1920) was founded on the assumption of interpersonally comparable and cardinal welfares. Robbins (1932) criticized this notion, arguing that interpersonal comparisons of utility were not possible. He cast doubt on the possibility of verifying whether the utility that one person gained from a particular state could be compared with the utility of another person from an alternative state. This led to attempts to concentrate on ordinal rather than cardinal utility. Arrow (1963) proposed four desirable criteria for social choice based on ordinal preferences. These were an unrestricted domain, preferences independent of irrelevant alternatives, weak Pareto principle satisfied and no dictatorship. Arrow's 'impossibility theorem' proved that no SWF based on ordinal utility satisfies these four criteria.[7]

This has led to an extensive debate on the degree of interpersonal comparability that can be assumed and an emphasis in the literature on partial cardinal unit comparability. Economists such as Mirrlees (1971) and Ng (1983) have argued for the inclusion of interpersonal comparability in welfare analysis. However, there is a divergence of opinion on the acceptable extent of comparability. The various degrees of comparability have been classified by Sen (1977) and Roberts (1980a, 1980b).[8] Cardinal unit comparability assumes that changes in welfare can be measured in comparable units, despite the fact that it is not possible to determine the level of each individual's utility. Interpersonal comparability with cardinality is required if we do not want to impose any limitations to introducing distributional concerns (Sen 1974).

The application of non-market valuation techniques to the estimation of distributional preferences requires the assumption of a degree of interpersonal comparability. This does not imply that one person is able to put herself in the other's place and have full information about their level of well-being. Crucially, though, it does assume that each person has an SWF that reflects his or her personal distributional preferences.

Determination of the SWF is also dependent on assumptions made about whether an individual's utility is determined solely by self-gratification. If the notion of altruism is included, it can be assumed that the individual's utility depends not only on the goods and services that she receives from the market or government sector of the economy, but also on the consumption and production activities of others. In this instance a person's utility arises from an awareness of what is happening to others.[9] This altruistic utility interdependence can be expressed in the following manner:

$$U_i = u_i(X_i, X_j, U_j) \qquad (2.4)$$

where U_i is the utility of the *i*th person, which depends on the magnitude of:

X_i, the amount of all n goods consumed by the ith person, X_j, the amount of all these n goods consumed by the jth person or persons, and U_j, the utility levels of other individuals or groups (Mishan 1981).

This highlights an important distinction between interdependent utility, where the utility or well-being of one individual is reflected in the utility function of another, and the social ranking of individuals, where each individual ranks the utility of various individuals or groups in his or her personal social welfare ranking. If estimation of distributional preferences is dependent on the assumption that respondents are maximizing a social welfare function dependent on individual utilities, this must be distinguished from utility maximization where altruistic preferences may be displayed.

2.1.3 Measuring Welfare Changes

Assessment of policy options involves analysis of comparisons of changes in welfare. Consequently it is the estimation of welfare changes, and in particular of changes in the SWF in moving from one resource allocation to another, that is of relevance. This involves estimating the utility of each individual in each state and aggregating the utilities to the SWF. The following method of explaining the measurement of welfare changes is adapted from Johansson (1993).

Assume an economy with i individuals, each demanding n goods and supplying k factors traded in markets. Within the context of environmental policy, it is also assumed that each individual demands an unpriced environmental asset denoted environmental quality, and each individual has a fixed lump sum income. The indirect utility function of individual, i, is written as:

$$V_i = v_i(p, w, y_i, z) \tag{2.5}$$

where V_i is the utility level attained, $p = [p_1,...,p_n]$ is a vector of prices of private goods, $w = [w_1,...,w_k]$ is a vector of wage rates, y_i is a lump-sum income including profit income but less any taxes, and z denotes environmental quality. It is assumed that the indirect utility function has an inverse relationship with price and a positive relationship with the wage rate, lump sum income and the quality of the environment.[10]

The problem facing the individual can be viewed as either a constrained maximization problem, in terms of maximizing utility within a budget constraint, or a constrained minimization problem in terms of minimizing expenditure while maintaining a particular level of utility. Hence, the measurement of utility (u_i) can also be expressed as an expenditure function, that is:

$$E_i = e_i(p, w, u_i, z) \tag{2.6}$$

As both the expenditure function and the indirect utility function are used in later equations, the relationship between the two is specified.

$$v_i(p, w, y_i, z) = V_i \Leftrightarrow e_i(p, w, u_i, z) = E_i \qquad (2.7)$$

By aggregating the indirect utility functions, the SWF may be written as:

$$W = w(V_1, \ldots V_n) = W[v_1(p, w, y_i, z_1), \ldots v_n(p, w, y_i, z_n)] \qquad (2.8)$$

This is a useful manipulation, as the measurement of social welfare can be approached by an aggregation of the money metric measure of utilities rather than the utilities themselves.

While the expenditure function can be used as a base to estimate indirect utility, estimates of changes in welfare are required in order to embody both equity and efficiency considerations in decision making. Hicks (1943) refined four measures of consumer welfare changes. These are compensating variation (CV), compensating surplus (CS), equivalent variation (EV) and equivalent surplus (ES). Pearce (1976) and Hanley and Spash (1993) provide succinct summaries of these consumer surplus measures.[11] The compensating surplus (CS) and equivalent surplus (ES) are two measures that are based on the indirect utility function and the expenditure function and are generally used to emphasize the change in the provision of a public good.

The compensating surplus (CS) for an environmental improvement is defined by Freeman (2003) as the maximum sum of money an individual would be willing to pay rather than do without the improvement. Similarly, utility changes can be expressed in terms of an ES; this is the minimum sum of money an individual would require to voluntarily forgo the improvement (Freeman 2003). The CS can be applied following changes in environmental quality and is often interpreted as the willingness to pay (WTP) for an improvement (Johansson 1993). The CS is also used to measure the WTP for a change in the quantity supplied of a public good. Concentrating on the CS for the moment, it can be expressed in terms of the expenditure function:[12]

$$CS_i = e_i(p, w, u_i, z_1) - e_i(p, w, u_i, z_2) + \Delta m \qquad (2.9)$$

where Δm is the change in income resulting from a policy change that affects environmental quality. The CS and ES provide a measure of the utility change for an individual; the next step is determining an aggregate for measuring utility changes in the community.

2.1.4 Deriving the Distributional Weight

A change in policy that moves the economy from an initial equilibrium, denoted by a subscript 0, to another, denoted by a subscript 1, will make everyone better off if:

$$v_i(p_0, w_0, y_{0i}, z_1) > v_i(p_0, w_0, y_{0i}, z_0) \quad \forall i \tag{2.10}$$

Although this outcome will pass the Pareto test, it is unrealistic, as most projects will make some individuals better off and others worse off. In this instance:

$$v_i(p_0, w_0, y_{0i}, z_1) > v_i(p_0, w_0, y_{0i}, z_0) \quad \exists i \in \eta \tag{2.11}$$

$$v_i(p_0, w_0, y_{0i}, z_1) < v_i(p_0, w_0, y_{0i}, z_0) \quad \exists i \in \eta \tag{2.12}$$

where η is the set of individuals. Hence there is a need for a principle other than the Pareto principle to rank outcomes involving both winners and losers. This is provided by an SWF, Equation (2.8), which can be written as indicated earlier:

$$W = w(V_1, \dots V_n) = W[v_1(p, w, y_i, z_1), \dots v_n(p, w, y_i, z_n)] \tag{2.8}$$

Hence, the social welfare function is a function of the utility levels of all individuals such that a higher value of welfare is preferred to a lower one. The impact of a project on social welfare is the change in welfare denoted by:

$$\begin{aligned} \Delta W = &w[v_1(p_1, w_1, y_{1i}, z_1), \dots v_n(p_1, w_1, y_{ni}, z_n)] \\ &- w[v_i(p_0, w_0, y_{0i}, z_0), \dots v_n(p_0, w_0, y_{ni}, z_n)] \end{aligned} \tag{2.13}$$

where the superscripts 0 and 1 reflect the initial and final values respectively. Although the individual utility levels are unobservable, this problem is overcome by calculating money measures of individual utility changes as indicated in the expenditure function. Thus:

$$v_i(p_0, w_0, y_{0i} - CS_i, z_1) = v_i(p_0, w_0, y_{0i}, z_0) \quad \forall i \tag{2.14}$$

$$v_i(p_0, w_0, y_{0i}, z_1) = v_i(p_0, w_0, y_{0i} + ES_i, z_0) \quad \forall i \tag{2.15}$$

where CS_i denotes the compensating surplus (Equation 2.9) and ES_i the equivalent surplus for individual i. Concentrating on the compensating surplus and substituting Equation (2.14) into Equation (2.13), the change in social welfare can be written as:

$$\Delta W = w[v_1(p_1, w_1, y_{1i}, z_1), \dots v_n(p_1, w_1, y_{ni}, z_n)]$$
$$- w[v_i(p_1, w_1, y_{1i} - CS_i, z_1), \dots v_n(p_1, w_1, y_{ni} - CS_n, z_n)] \qquad (2.16)$$

$$= \sum_{i=1}^{n} \int_0^{CS_i} W_i V_{iy} \, dCS_i = \sum_{i=1}^{n} (\overline{W_i V_{iy}}) CS_i \qquad (2.17)$$

where $W_i = \partial W/\partial V_i$, $V_{iy} = \partial V_i/\partial y_i$ and a bar indicates that the intermediate value theorem has been used to find an average value for $W_i V_{iy}$ between initial and final values such that equality of the equation is maintained.

This shows that, for each individual, the change in welfare resulting from a particular project can be measured by calculating the product of the individual's average social utility of income and his/her compensating surplus. The community change in social welfare is determined by summing the resulting amount for all individuals. Hence, the change in welfare is a *weighted aggregate* of the compensating surpluses.

2.1.5 Interpreting the Distributional Weight

The distributional weighting term is known as either the marginal social utility of income (Johansson 1993) or, more generally, the marginal social utility (Boadway and Bruce 1984). We will use the term *distributional weight* to refer to the weighting term as defined. This distributional weight is dependent on two components: the change in social welfare if the utility or well-being of individual i increases marginally ($\partial W/\partial V_i$) and the marginal utility of income of individual i ($\partial V_i/\partial y_i$).

The first component of the weight, ($\partial W/\partial V_i$), is the marginal social welfare attributed to individual i. It indicates how the person whose social welfare preferences are being reflected ranks the utility of individual i in their distributional preferences. For example, in their view, is social welfare enhanced or diminished if the utility of a low-income person is improved relative to a high-income person? In practice, social justice preferences will most likely be expressed in terms of groups within society who share common characteristics rather than individuals. Rawls (1971) suggests that public debate is frequently framed in terms of groups rather than individuals. Hence, in eliciting the distributional preferences of the community, it is more practical to think in terms of groups who share a common characteristic. Examples of characteristics which may influence these perceptions include age, income, ethnicity, race or geography.

The second component of the weight, ($\partial V_i/\partial y_i$), is the marginal utility of income of individual i. It reflects the assessment, by the person whose welfare preferences are being reflected, of how the utility of individual i changes as a result of an increase in income. For example, is the view held that an extra dollar would increase the utility of a low-income person more than it would increase the utility of a high-income person? Although this component of the weight is often referred to in terms of income, this does not need to be the case. For example, it could also refer to the marginal utility of an additional unit of an environmental good for individual *i*. Medin et al. (2001) illustrate the sensitivity of distributional weights to the choice of numéraire, acknowledging that utility is dependent upon a broader range of factors than income alone. This sensitivity is an area where further research is required to provide empirical estimates of the sensitivity of distributional weights to the choice of numéraire.

2.1.6 The Shape of the SWF

The functional form of the SWF involves ethical judgements about how to aggregate individual utilities. These judgements are evident in the distributional weights. They reflect varying theories of social justice. For example, in a Benthamite or classical utilitarian society, all changes in utility are treated equally. This is not the same as an egalitarian society where weights are applied with the aim of an equal outcome. Alternatively, in a Rawlsian society, weights for all except the worst-off are equal to zero, reflecting Rawls's view that welfare is maximized by seeking to maximize the utility of the least well-off group. Due to the assumption that the SWF is increasing with each individual's utility level, as outlined in section 2.1.1, the distributional weights cannot be negative (Cowell and Gardiner 1999).

The willingness to trade off the utility or well-being of one individual for another is reflected in the slope of the SWF and is known as the *social marginal rate of substitution (SMRS)*. The SMRS is influenced by the two identified components of the distributional weights. Figure 2.1 illustrates some of the more well known forms of the SWF.[13] The convex function in Figure 2.1a assumes that the SMRS is diminishing with movement down the SWF. This assumes that as the utility of individual 1 (V_1) increases, the holder of the SWF is willing to trade less of the well-being of individual 2 (V_2) for an additional increase in the utility of individual 1. In some instances the further restriction of constant elasticity is imposed (Cowell and Gardiner 1999; Pearce 2006). Figure 2.1b depicts a classical utilitarian SWF where the utility of each individual is treated equally, resulting in the utility of different individuals being regarded as perfect substitutes. In Figure 2.1c a Rawlsian SWF is illustrated where social welfare does not increase unless the utility of the least well-off individual increases.

a) Diminishing SMRS

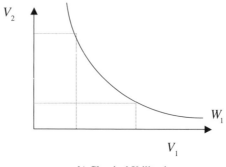

b) Classical Utilitarian

c) Rawlsian

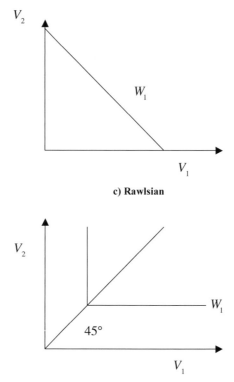

Source: Adapted from Johansson (1993, pp. 18–19).

Figure 2.1 Social welfare functions

In summary, a distributional weighting term can be derived by assuming that each individual is able to rank alternative social states and that their preferences can be expressed in the form of an SWF. The magnitude of the distributional weight is dependent on:

- the holder of the SWF's assessment of the impact of money or access to goods and services on the utility of other individuals in society, and
- the impact of changes in the utility of other individuals in society on the SWF of the person whose welfare preferences are being reflected. In effect, each member of the community holds preferences with respect to their personal judgment regarding social justice.

Hence, an assumption of equal distributional weights implies first, that the marginal utility of consumption for all individuals in society is considered equal and, second, that a marginal change in well-being for each individual in society is regarded equally. Given the likely variance in individuals' distributional preferences, it is unlikely that distributional weights will always be equal. Yet, if no distributional weights are applied in a CBA, the unrealistic assumptions of equal marginal utility and marginal welfare are being applied by default.

2.2 APPLYING DISTRIBUTIONAL WEIGHTS IN COST–BENEFIT ANALYSIS

One well-established application of the theory of measuring welfare changes using the SWF is CBA.[14] CBA measures, in monetary units, how social welfare is affected by a particular policy, thereby providing a practical guide to social decision-making. Randall (2002, p. 53) asserts that:

> In the past half century, benefit-cost analysis has evolved from a relatively crude financial feasibility analysis for capital-intensive public works (water resources and transportation projects were early applications in several countries) to a sophisticated and comprehensive application of the economic-theoretic principles of welfare change measurement to evaluate all manner of projects, programs, and policies.

CBA is founded on the assumption that a policy is worthwhile for society as a whole if the benefits (B) exceed the costs (C). That is, the discounted net social benefit must be greater than zero, as follows:

$$\sum_{t=1}^{T} (Bt - Ct) / [(1-s)^t > 0]) \tag{2.18}$$

where t represents the time period and s the discount rate.

The Kaldor–Hicks criterion, where it is assumed that those who gain can compensate those who lose, defines all policies with sums of benefits exceeding sums of costs as socially beneficial.[15]

The benefits of a policy are measured by the sum total of the willingness to pay (WTP) or willingness to accept compensation (WTA) of each individual in the community. Each individual expresses his or her preferences through their WTP or WTA. Table 2.1 summarizes the relationship between WTP, WTA and the compensating and equivalent surpluses introduced in section 2.1.3.

Table 2.1 Relationship between WTP, WTA and compensating and equivalent surpluses

Technical name of the measure of consumer's surplus	Context: the policy benefits the individual	Context: the policy makes the individual worse off
Compensating surplus	WTP for the project	WTA for tolerating the project
Equivalent surplus	WTA to forgo the project	WTP to avoid the project

Source: Adapted from Pearce and Barbier (2000, p. 52).

For a traded good, marginal WTP is reflected in the market price. For non-market goods, such as clean air or the preservation of wildlife, it may need to be estimated. There are a number of ways in which this can be measured.[16]

The costs of a policy can generally be measured using competitive market prices. This is the price at which producers are willing to supply a good or service. The supply price reflects the opportunity cost, or the value of the next best alternative use, of the resources used to produce that input. Shadow prices may also be used to estimate costs in cases where prices are distorted.[17]

Equity considerations can be incorporated into the measurement of CBA by weighting the utility changes derived from benefits and costs. If distributional weights as derived in section 2.1.4 are incorporated into a CBA analysis, then the distributional or equity effects of a project are considered along with efficiency considerations. Attaching weights to the groups of the people who are reaping the benefits or bearing the costs can be incorporated as follows:

$$W = \alpha_1 U_1 + \alpha_2 U_2 + \alpha_3 U_3 + \ldots + \alpha_n U_n \qquad (2.19)$$

where the distributional weights are given by the αs and the utility to each group given by U_{1-n}. Pearce (2006) labels this SWF a 'generalisable utilitarian' SWF or 'weighted sum of utilities' SWF. The following example, taken from Pearce (2006), can be used to illustrate the application of distributional weights in CBA. In panel A of Table 2.2, a conventional CBA is summarized where those who gain can compensate those who lose and the final net gain of +2 indicates support for this policy. In panel B, when, for example, Group B may be low-income earners and Group A high-income earners, distributional weights of $\alpha_B = 1.6$ and $\alpha_A = 1.0$ are applied and the CBA approach suggests that the policy should be rejected. Without weights, aggregation is the sum of the benefits of a policy change (that is, the sum of the compensating surpluses) but this is not a measure of the change in social welfare because of the underlying assumption that the distributional weights are equal for all individuals or groups.

Table 2.2 Applying distributional weights in CBA

Panel A: Comparison of unweighted gains and losses			
	Gain	Loss	Net gain
Group A	+10	−4	+6
Group B	+2	−6	−4
Aggregate gain	+12	−10	+2

Panel B: Comparison of weighted gains and losses			
	Gain	Loss	Net gain
Group A	+10	−4	+6
Group B	+2 × 1.6 = +3.2	−6 × 1.6 = −9.6	−6.4
Aggregate gain	+13.2	−13.6	−0.4

Source: Pearce (2006, p. 63).

2.2.1 The Application of Distributional Weights in Practice

Despite the rigorous theoretical foundations in applied CBA, there are few examples where the individual compensating or equivalent surpluses have been weighted (Adler and Posner 1999).[18] In order to assess why distributional weights are not generally applied, the application of CBA has been separated into two areas: the use of CBA for project appraisal from a development economics stance, and the assessment of projects at a national level from a public policy perspective.

From an economic development perspective, two seminal works which incorporated discussion of distributional weights in terms of project evaluation at a global level were Little and Mirrlees (1974) and Squire and van der Tak (1975). These authors were concerned with the need to consider the effect on global income distribution in assessing the costs and benefits of development projects. The assumption was that less weight should be attached to the consumption of a rich person than that of a poor person. The World Bank version of the methodology of project evaluation was published in Squire and van der Tak (1975). This methodology incorporated 'social' prices, where consumption was weighted according to the income of the consumer. At about the same time, Little and Mirlees (1974) published their approach to shadow pricing, where distributional weights were also incorporated. 'A battle raged in the World Bank during the 1970s about whether social prices should be used. Formally, the "social price brigade" won, in that guidelines on the use of distributional weights were actually incorporated in the Operational Manual in 1980' (Little and Mirrlees 1994, p. 207).

However, in an article reflecting on their work 20 years later, Little and Mirrlees (1994) indicate their more general disappointment with the application of unweighted values in CBA for project appraisal by the World Bank. As indicated in the World Bank operations manual, distributional weights are generally still not applied in terms of project evaluation (World Bank 1996). Little and Mirrlees (1994) cite a number of reasons for this, largely to do with the politics of the World Bank, yet claim that their methods of project evaluation have survived analytical scrutiny and are capable of being used effectively.

From a public policy viewpoint, the application of CBA dates back to 1936 when the United States government directed agencies to estimate the costs and benefits of projects designed for flood control. However, in these early stages, equity issues were not considered, and agencies were directed to ignore the distribution of benefits and costs and give attention only to their total amounts (Kneese and Schulze 1985; Adler and Posner 1999). More recently, the approach to incorporating distributional weights in CBA varies across government financial decision-making bodies. For example, in the UK, HM Treasury has officially endorsed distributional weights in CBA as detailed in its Green Book (HM Treasury 2003). In Australia, the Commonwealth Department of Finance and Administration recommends that, as a general rule, distributional weights should not be assigned 'and that recommendations of cost–benefit analyses flag the need for distributional judgements to be made at the political level' (Department of Finance and Administration 2006).

This raises the issue of the distinction between the application of explicit or implicit distributional weights. Adler and Posner (1999) suggest that, at a national level in the US, if distributional weights are applied, the weighting appears to be made implicitly through the policy decision-making process.[19]

Earlier examples of where implicit weights have been applied in policy decision are documented by Haveman (1965) and Weisbrod (1972).

Campbell and Brown (2003) suggest that, while in an ideal situation distributional weighting would be undertaken across all public-sector projects being appraised and evaluated, in the real world the project analyst is most likely operating in a vacuum with respect to national guidelines regarding distribution. Adler and Posner (1999) provide a summary of the dilemma facing policy-makers and economists that is reflected in the literature. One branch of the literature proposes that economists should evaluate projects on the basis of SWFs that include proper distributional weightings. Utility is assumed to be cardinal under this approach; different people's utility can be weighted and summed. Adler and Posner (1999) conclude that this approach is intellectually rigorous, but it is not useful because it is too demanding on the decision-maker and agencies do not use such ambitious SWFs in the real world. The other branch of the literature holds that economists should evaluate projects on the basis of unweighted costs and benefits. This approach, which assumes that the marginal social value of a dollar is the same regardless of the household or individual that receives it, has had more influence. 'The pure approach is impractical; the practical approach impure. It is relatively straightforward to aggregate CVs, but the outcome does not necessarily reveal whether a project enhances welfare' (Adler and Posner 1999, p. 193).

2.2.2 The Estimation of Distributional Weights

A review of the literature suggests that one of the dominant reasons for the reluctance of practitioners to embrace distributional weights within CBA is the difficulty in estimating weights empirically. Authors such as Mishan (1981) and Harberger (1978) have argued that distribution should not be a part of CBA, with one of their main contentions being the difficulty in determining the weights to be applied. A number of methods for estimating distributional weights have been discussed in the literature. For example, 'value sensitive analysis' refers to situations where the analyst determines the weights (Nash et al. 1975). However, Mishan (1988) expressed concern that, if economists choose weights, this will reflect only one view of the appropriate weights and runs the risk of discrediting CBA as a technique. This ignores the fact that, in the absence of distributional analysis from economists, policy-makers may be confronted with the need to apply their own implicit weights.

Another alternative discussed by Mishan (1981) is that weights be determined from the political process. However, he proposes that the continual changes this would involve would create instability. A further concern is the possibility that political interventions would be difficult to limit and that these weights may simply reflect the power of specific vested interest groups rather than a reflection of society's marginal social utility for different groups. The 'revisionist' school (Dasgupta et al. 1972; Little and Mirrlees 1974) refers to studies where weights are derived from the political system and where the major application has been in developed countries. However, experience has shown that this method of determining weights has been slow to develop.

Another proposal has been that distributional weights be determined by the progressive tax schedule (Harberger 1978). This concept has been further developed by Yitzhaki (2003) who proposes adopting the framework of the theory of tax reform as the basic tool of analysis.[20] These methods may ensure consistency in value judgements, however their major limitation is that distributional weights based on the marginal utility of income do not allow for the fact that utility may be based on other criteria, such as environment.

It may also be possible to estimate weights based on an analysis of past decisions. Basu (1980) clearly elaborates the difficulties in using revealed preferences to determine governmental weights. Compounding the estimation complication is the theoretical argument that past decisions have not necessarily maximized welfare.

Hence, although the theory of applying distributional weights in CBA has progressed, the practicality of determining appropriate distributional weights has remained unresolved. The difficulty of incorporating equity in CBA is not defining weights in principle, but their estimation in practice. It is this need which has given rise to this book and to the development of non-market valuation techniques to address the question of estimating distributional weights suitable for inclusion in a CBA setting.

2.2.3 Further Difficulties with the Application of Distributional Weights

Beyond the problem of estimation, several other concerns have been raised in the literature regarding the efficacy of applying distributional weights in CBA. Foremost in this discussion is the extent of the efficiency trade-off to be made in exchange for incorporating equity considerations in policy analysis. If it is assumed that the incorporation of weights in CBA is possible, then the subsequent question is: with full knowledge of these equity issues, are we prepared to forfeit efficiency in the quest for incorporating increased equity considerations? Harberger (1978, 1984) provides an example to illustrate his opposition to the application of distributional weights. Assume a desert country where people live on oases, some of them rich and some poor. The proposed project is sending ice cream on camelback across the desert. If the recipient oasis has a distributional weight equal to four times that of the sending oasis, then the project would be acceptable even if up to three-quarters of the ice cream melted and was lost en route. This example clearly illustrates the need to take into account the possible efficiency cost associated with the incorporation of equity considerations.

However, more recently, Johansson-Stenman (2005) shows a large range of cases when the application of distributional weights provides optimal outcomes. His analysis suggests that the commonly expressed perception that using distributional weights generally implies large efficiency losses 'appears to be incorrect, or strongly misleading at best'.

With the cost of the distributional transfers being important in the efficiency/ equity trade-off, the debate becomes whether the taxation system is the most cost-effective manner of implementing distributional transfers or whether public-sector projects are also an efficient means of achieving some equity goals. This depends to some degree on the extent of the development of the tax and welfare systems. In less developed countries, in some circumstances, the only acceptable method of making transfers may be via public-sector projects to provide social infrastructure such as schools and hospitals, or economic infrastructure such as roads and irrigation facilities. Drèze (1998) asserts that it is wishful thinking to assume that distributional concerns can be adequately dealt with through taxes, transfers and related policy instruments. Furthermore, Brent (1991) asserts that even if inefficient projects are approved, this does not necessarily imply a policy contradiction. If weighted benefits exceed weighted costs, then society is better off and welfare is maximized with the project. In effect, the weights reflect the trade-off between efficiency and distribution which is central to public policy. As it is not realistic to expect that policies will be both efficient and distributionally fair, specifying the weights results in transparency of value judgements about the trade-off between efficiency and equity.

Mishan (1988) suggests that, no matter how accurate or acceptable the distributional weights, the incorporation of weights will not serve the purpose of promoting equity. However, the incorporation of distributional weights means that even if a project that impacts on the distribution of welfare does go ahead, it is with increased knowledge of the distributional consequences.[21] As Kriström (2006) observes, acknowledgement of the distributional impacts does not imply that policy-makers have to aspire for equity. Instead, it means the inclusion of distributional effects in policy analysis. The inclusion of distributional weights in CBA addresses a need to incorporate both efficiency and equity criteria into the decision-making calculus. The issue then becomes whether the weights are implicit or explicit. We promote an explicit approach.

Aligned with the question of the potential efficiency cost of incorporating equity in policy analysis is the question of whether issues related to equity are within the realm of economics. Writers such as Sagoff (1988) believe that it is the role of the political process, and not of economic analysis, to judge the opinions and beliefs of the community which are central to legislation. Hence, he believes that CBA 'gets beyond itself, treading on ground to which its character and procedures are ill suited' (Belshaw 2001, p. 60). Fundamental to this criticism is the question of whether individual preferences on which economists rely actually reflect ethical and value judgements. These criticisms fail to acknowledge the distinction within economic theory between an individual maximizing a utility function and a social welfare function as specified in this chapter. Hence, in estimating an SWF, individuals express their preferences for welfare outcomes from a wider perspective than that assumed of the consumer. The social welfare preferences reflected in distributional weights are different from individual utility-maximizing preferences. They reflect each individual's personal distributional preferences, as reflected in his or her SWF.

2.2.4 Why Incorporate Distributional Weights in CBA?

If the aim of CBA is to provide a ranking of policy proposals, the analysis of policy options requires a consideration of both efficiency and equity implications. One of the main reasons why distributional considerations have not been included more frequently is the reluctance of economists and policymakers to become involved in normative decisions. In fact, Weisbrod (1972) suggested that the tendency to distinguish between equity and efficiency considerations has led to the connotation of efficiency questions being 'economic' and 'scientific' and equity considerations being 'non-economic' and 'non-scientific'. Sutherland (2006, p. 171) also suggests that distributional considerations are less often considered as there is 'no commonly accepted definition of optimum equity; certainly nothing analogous to maximum net benefits from economic efficiency'.

Yet, given that policy options create changes in community welfare, any process for evaluating policy options needs to attempt to measure changes in welfare. CBA will not achieve this if distributional considerations are ignored. This leads Drèze (1998) to conclude that 'there is no plausible alternative to the use of distributional weights'. The inclusion of distributional weights enables the policy-maker to be more fully informed about both the equity and the efficiency consequences of a project. Without the application of distributional weights, the implicit assumption is that the marginal social value of income and/or consumption is equal for everyone. This therefore implies that the current distribution of income and goods and services is optimal (Pearce 1983). Hence, by default, the conventional CBA, where no weights are used, treats each benefit or cost with a weight of one – regardless of who receives the benefit or incurs the cost.

If we assume that no knowledge of distributional weights is made available through a CBA, then the value judgements upon which decisions are finally made will often be left to the discretion of the policy-maker or to political processes. This diminishes the transparency of the decision-making process.

Furthermore, as Campbell and Brown (2003) reinforce, assuming that the distribution of a project's benefits and costs does not matter is as much a value judgement as the situation in which we assume that distribution does matter.

Policy interventions have to be sensitive to the winners and losers, not only because that matters from a social justice point of view, but also because the political acceptability and effectiveness of the measures will depend on the distribution of the costs and benefits. Possibly the most cogent reason for being concerned with distribution is that an understanding of distributional impacts allows the shaping of policy packages that are more likely to be accepted by the public (Kriström 2006).

To summarize, the difficulties associated with the practical application of distributional weights in CBA suggest that one of the key impediments to the incorporation of equity preferences in policy analysis has been the question of estimating social justice preferences. We address this question by illustrating the application of a non-market valuation technique to the estimation of distributional weights.

2.3 CONCLUSIONS

This chapter has outlined the concept of distributional weights in a welfare economics theoretical setting. Based on the assumption that each individual's distributional preferences can be expressed in the form of an SWF, the measurement of welfare changes arising from policy alternatives can be undertaken by estimating the weighted aggregate compensating surpluses. We review the theory that the distributional weights are dependent on two components: the marginal change in welfare arising from the change in utility to an individual and the marginal change in utility to the individual arising from a change in consumption or income.

Failure to incorporate distributional weighting in CBA results in the application of the assumptions that both the marginal social welfare and the marginal utility of income of consumption are equal for all individuals in society. This illustrates the disparity between the conceptual progress and the practical application with respect to incorporating equity in policy analysis. Observation of empirical policy assessment within public policy and project evaluation shows that explicit distributional weights are not generally applied. A number of obstacles associated with the incorporation of equity in policy analysis have been identified and include the likely trade-off between efficiency and equity objectives and the determination of appropriate distributional weights.

However, foremost amongst the hurdles to applying distributional weights in practice are the difficulties in the elicitation and determination of distributional preferences. As a result, the focus of the rest of this book is on the development of choice modelling as a technique for estimating distributional preferences.

NOTES

1. Authors such as Broome (1995) dispute the validity of this assumption. He cites, for example, a drug user who may not be the best judge of his/her own welfare and that society's acceptance of this is reflected in public policy in this area.
2. The anthropocentric view of economists, where welfare is based on preference satisfaction, is rejected by authors such as Sagoff (1988).
3. This is not without criticism. For example, Sen (2000) suggests that the focus should be on functionings and capabilities.
4. Although, traditionally, economists have assumed utility to be dependent on consumption alone, more recent authors such as Ekins (2000) and the ecological economics literature suggest that utility is generated by many other aspects of life which can be broadly classified by modes of experience: that is, being, having, doing and interacting.
5. This assumption is discussed in greater detail in Chapter 4 as it is not applied in the case study CM application.
6. Mueller (1989) provides the proof that the impartial utilitarian chooses a distribution of income such that the marginal utility of income across all individuals is equal.
7. For proof, see Arrow (1984).
8. For further elaboration, see the table of alternatives on p. 53 of Myles (1995).
9. This can be distinguished from externalities which arise from a direct or physical effect on another.
10. For further elaboration of the properties of this function, see Johansson (1993, p. 42). Other useful references include Boadway and Bruce (1984), Drèze and Stern (1987), and Johansson (1987, 1993).
11. A movement along the demand curve reflects two responses. The reduction in price induces both a substitution and an income effect: the substitution effect because consumers are induced to substitute the now relatively cheaper good for other goods, even if real income is unchanged; the income effect because of the change in consumption as a result of the increase in purchasing power.
12. See Boadway and Bruce (1984, p. 202) for further detail.
13. Note that these SWFs reflect inequality in terms of unit of utility. This does not indicate indifference to inequality of income or consumption, because the marginal utility derived from an additional unit of consumption may vary between individuals (Johansson 1991).
14. Hanley and Spash (1993, p. 5) provide a chronology of the development of CBA in the US dating back to 1808.
15. The sum of net benefits is not a necessary and sufficient condition for a project to pass the compensation test, in general. This is known as the 'Boadway Paradox', derived by Boadway (1974). Blackorby and Donaldson (1990) provide an example.
16. For further detail on methods of non-market valuation, see, for example, Garrod and Willis (1999) or Bateman et al. (2002).
17. Drèze and Stern (1994, p. 59) define shadow prices as the 'social opportunity costs of the resources used and correspondingly for outputs generated'.
18. One example is Blackorby and Donaldson (1987). They analyse a method for distributionally sensitive CBA that uses household welfare ratios (the ratio of household income to the appropriate poverty line) as an index of each household member's well-being. Although this has a number of advantages, it is limited in that focusing on income is a constrained indicator of well-being.
19. For an example, see Adler and Posner (1999, pp. 173–4) and their conclusion about the Environmental Protection Authority and agricultural pesticides.
20. Brent (2006) illustrates the potential applicability of Yitzhaki's criterion with respect to assessing China's accession to the World Trade Organisation.
21. Harberger (1984) suggests an alternative approach that he calls the 'basic needs approach'. In this case it is recipients' consumption of particular goods or services (food, education, medical care, etc.) or attainments of certain states (being better nourished, better educated, etc.) that are closely correlated with an 'adequate' consumption of such goods and services. However, a problem with the basic needs approach is that it does not assist in evaluating the social and economic impacts of policy options.

3. Choice modelling and distributional preferences

3.0 INTRODUCTION

The welfare economics theory discussed in Chapter 2 suggests that, in theory, the notion of including distributional weights in CBA is theoretically sound. However, in practice, incorporating distributional weights is not a common approach among policy-makers. As discussed, this partly reflects the difficulties associated with the empirical estimation of distributional preferences. This chapter addresses this question by introducing the stated preference method of choice modelling as a way to estimate the distributional or equity preferences of the community. Choice modelling is a quantitative statistical method that has been steadily developing since the 1970s and has conventionally been applied to problems of non-market valuation.

3.1 CHOICE MODELLING

Choice modelling is a form of conjoint analysis; meaning that alternatives are considered jointly or simultaneously. Conjoint methods include: choice modelling, contingent ranking, contingent rating and paired comparisons. Although choice modelling has only been used relatively recently in environmental valuation exercises (Adamowicz et al. 1994; Roe et al. 1996), it has been employed by psychologists since the 1960s and in transportation and marketing research since the early 1970s (Garrod and Willis 1999). From these beginnings, the method has evolved through advances in a variety of disciplines where the common goal has been the development of a method to explain individual and aggregate choice behaviour. Louviere et al. (2000), Haab and McConnell (2002), Bennett and Blamey (2001) and Hensher et al. (2005) provide valuable explanations and discussions of the methodology and application of choice modelling.

Choice modelling is designed to study the choices people make and to understand the behavioural processes that lead to particular choices. Choice modelling differs from typical conjoint methods in that individual respondents are asked to choose from alternative bundles of attributes instead of ranking or rating them (Adamowicz et al. 1998). The approach was initially developed by Louviere and Hensher (1982) and Louviere and Woodworth (1983).

Conventionally, choice modelling has been used to estimate non-market values. Stated preference techniques, such as choice modelling, rely on eliciting consumer preferences through some form of questionnaire approach. The main alternative category of methods used to estimate non-market values are revealed preference methods, such as hedonic pricing and the travel-cost method, where value estimations are based on the actual behaviour of consumers.[1]

Aside from choice modelling, the other well-known stated preference valuation technique is contingent valuation. This method generally involves asking survey respondents what they would be willing to pay for a benefit, based on hypothetical terms under which it would be provided.[2] Although contingent valuation has developed considerably (Mitchell and Carson 1995), there has been debate over its application because of the scepticism associated with relying on what respondents say they will do compared with how they might actually behave. Bennett (2005) reflects that one impetus for the development of choice modelling was the controversy about the use of contingent valuation which followed the debate surrounding the Exxon Valdez oil-spill compensation case in the United States, and the Coronation Hill mining case in Australia. Although choice modelling is also a stated preference method and therefore also subject to limitations regarding divergence between stated and actual behaviour, one of its strengths is its emphasis on reinforcing to respondents the constraints within which decision-making takes place. Morrison et al. (1996) provide a useful comparison of the strengths and weaknesses of the contingent valuation and choice modelling methods of non-market valuation.

In traditional applications, choice modelling is used to identify the utility that certain attributes of goods or services have for individuals by examining the trade-offs implicit in consumption choices. This provides the flexibility to predict behavioural responses to changing opportunities. Respondents are presented with a set of alternatives known as a choice set. For example, in a transport study, the set may comprise alternatives such as travelling by car, bus or train. Choice modelling mimics actual behaviour because respondents make choices within a specified choice set (Kriström and Laitila 2003). Each alternative is described by attributes. In the foregoing transport example, these may be factors such as comfort, reliability and travel time. By varying the levels of the scenario attributes and observing respondents' preferred choices, it is possible to understand their preferences and the trade-offs they make between attributes. In particular, using one attribute to describe the costs associated with a policy alternative enables estimates of willingness to pay for particular attributes to be made. The two sources of influences on choice behaviour are the attributes describing an alternative and the characteristics of the respondent.

One of the strengths of choice modelling is that it forces respondents to consider substitution possibilities. Hence, the method is useful not only as a value estimation technique but also for assessing policy options. By presenting respondents with a description of alternative policy options and seeking an indication of the single preferred option, policy preferences can be elicited. For example, in a study of water supply policy alternatives, Blamey et al. (1999) illustrate how choice modelling can be used to provide both value estimates corresponding to policy changes involving one or more attributes and community rankings of multiple policy options.

Boxall et al. (1996) propose several other advantages of choice modelling as a research method. It provides a structure for respondents to be questioned in detail about a sample of events rather than a single event. It forces respondents to consider the trade-offs between attributes in each situation. And finally, the repeated sampling method employed in choice modelling alleviates some informational efficiency concerns, such as those associated with some contingent valuation methods which utilize two or three repeated measures from respondents.

Adamowicz et al. (1998) highlight the advantage of choice modelling for evaluating environmental losses. In the case of damage to a particular attribute, where respondents are forced to make trade-offs between attributes, compensating amounts of other goods can also be estimated. This may be more useful than compensating variation based on money. Adamowicz et al. (1999) stress the advantage that strategic behaviour by respondents should be minimal, as choices are made from descriptions of attributes and it will not be clear which choice will over- or under-represent a valuation. In comparison with revealed preference methods, stated preference methods such as choice modelling also have the advantage of being able to examine situations in terms of attributes and levels that do not exist in currently available options. Wills (2006, p. 189) suggests that choice modelling studies 'can alleviate the incentives for strategic distortions of valuations, and reduce the difficulties of understanding individual survey questions'.

Examples of the broad range of application of choice modelling within an environmental context include: the estimation of the environmental benefits of the Conversion of Cropland to Forest Grassland Program in China (Wang et al. 2006), the estimation of the value of changes in the deer-hunting season length in Ohio (Schwabe et al. 2001), the estimation of the environmental benefits from the allocation of water to the Macquarie Marshes in Australia (Bennett et al. 2001) and the estimation of consumers' willingness to pay for salmon of different colours (Alfnes et al. 2006).

The ability of choice modelling to value marginal changes in environmental attributes has also resulted in the values estimated using choice modelling being proposed for use in benefit transfer. Benefit transfer refers to the process of taking values from previous studies in other areas and applying them to the area where the new decision must be made (Kahn 2005). Morrison and Bergland (2006) show that, when sites and populations are similar, value estimates at policy and study sites are statistically equivalent. This supports the possibility for choice modelling values to be applied in benefit transfer.

3.1.1 Theoretical Background

Choice modelling derives from two theoretical foundations. First, it is based on the notion that utility is derived not from goods per se but rather from the characteristics which goods possess (Lancaster 1966, 1971). Rosen (1974) further developed the model for the case in which goods are indivisible. The approach allows the demand for, or value of, a particular attribute to be determined, assuming that a particular consumption service can be described by a set of attributes.

Second, random utility theory is used to estimate the probability of choice (Thurstone 1927). Random utility theory assumes that utility is a latent construct that exists (if at all) in the mind of the consumer, but cannot be observed directly by the researcher (Louviere 2001). The probability that a decision-maker will choose a particular alternative from a set of alternatives, given data observed by the researcher, can be calculated. As indicated, in most applications, each alternative is fully characterized by levels of attributes and a cost.

The random utility model is the basic model for analysing choice modelling responses. The econometric analysis is based on McFadden's conditional logit model (McFadden 1974), which was further developed by Hanemann (1984). With the conditional logit model, characteristics of the outcomes are used to predict the choice that is made (Long 1997). The closely related multinomial logit model (MNL), which is commonly estimated in choice modelling applications, allows the effects of independent variables to differ for each outcome. ('Multinomial' refers to the existence of two or more possible outcomes.) It can be thought of as simultaneously estimating binary logits for all possible comparisons among the outcome categories (Long 1997).

Under the analysis, it is assumed that individual, i, maximizes utility and that the indirect utility function (as introduced in Chapter 2), can be separated into two parts: an observable element which describes the preferences of individual, i, as a linear function of the goods attributes, X_q, and a stochastic element which represents those influences on individual choice which cannot be observed by the researcher. Hence, the indirect utility function for the ith individual of the qth alternative can be partitioned into two components, each a function of the characteristics of the alternative, X_q, and the characteristics of the individual, c_i:

$$U_{qi} = V_{qi}(X_q, c_i) + e_{qi}(X_q, c_i) \qquad (3.1)$$

where U_{qi} is the unobservable overall utility, V_{qi} is the observable objective component of utility and e_{qi} is the random component.

Different random utility models can be generated by allowing the random elements to enter the conditional indirect utility functions in different ways or by making different assumptions about their joint distribution. Consequently, two modelling decisions are required: the functional form of V_{qi} and the distribution of e_{qi}. Most approaches begin by specifying the utility function as additively separable in deterministic and stochastic preferences (Haab and McConnell 2002). In this case, V_{qi} is a conditional indirect utility function that is generally assumed to be linear in form:

$$V_{qi} = \beta_1 + \beta_{2i} x_{q2i} + \beta_{3i} x_{q3i} + \ldots + \beta_{qi} x_{qai} \qquad (3.2)$$

where x_{qai} are the attributes, $1 \ldots a$ of the specific alternative, q, and the vector contains the marginal utility parameters. In Equation (3.2), β_1 is the alternative-specific constant (ASC). The ASC represents the mean of the difference between the unobserved factors in the error term of one alternative and that of a base case. Data analysis entails estimation of the coefficient vector, β, which maximizes the probability of obtaining the observed choice. As Hensher et al. (2005) point out, the attributes may not necessarily enter the utility function in a linear form. For example, they may be specified in a logarithmic form, or as a quadratic. Interactions between attributes may also be specified and provide interesting results.

The unobserved component of the utility function, e_{qi}, requires careful definition. As the distribution of the unobserved sources of utility across the sampled population is unknown, some assumptions need to be introduced. Generally, two assumptions are made (Hensher et al. 2005): first, that the unobserved utility associated with each individual is located on some (unknown) distribution and randomly allocated to each sampled individual; and second, that each alternative has its own unobserved component within the distribution that defines the range of utility values.

The main selection probability axiom used to develop a basic operational model is known as the Independence from Irrelevant Alternatives (IIA) axiom.[3] This states that 'the ratio of the probabilities of choosing one alternative over another (given that both alternatives have a non-zero probability of choice) is unaffected by the presence or absence of any additional alternatives in the choice set' (Louviere et al. 2000, p. 44). The simplest starting assumption implied by the IIA axiom is that the set of unobserved components, while each having their own unique mean value, is independent with identical distributions. This set of assumptions is referred to as independently and identically distributed (IID) and follows the Gumbel or extreme value type I distribution,[4] and leads to the functional form for the utility expressions of the multinomial logit (MNL) model. The model which estimates the probability of individual i choosing alternative q can be expressed as:

$$P_{qi} = \frac{\exp(\mu V_{qi})}{\sum_{k=1}^{K} \exp(\mu V_{ki})} \quad (3.3)$$

As the V_{qi}s are assumed to be linear additive functions in the attributes which determine the utility of the qth alternative, then V_{qi} can be written as:

$$V_{qi} = \sum_{a=1}^{A} \mu \beta_{qi} X_{qai} \quad (3.4)$$

An estimate of the utility parameter, $\mu \beta_{qi}$, can be interpreted as an estimate of the weight of attribute, X_q, in the utility expression, V_q, of alternative q. In Equation (3.4), μ is a scale parameter which is inversely proportional to the standard deviation of the error distribution. In a single data set this parameter cannot be separately identified and is therefore implicit in the terms estimated. The maximum likelihood procedure also allows testing for statistical significance of individual utility parameters, or $\hat{\beta}$s, through calculation of the asymptotic standard errors for the $\hat{\beta}$s in the MNL model.

The MNL remains the most popular choice modelling framework and Louviere et al. (2000) speculate that, in part, this is due to its simplicity in estimation and its speed of delivering 'good' or 'acceptable' models on the accepted tests of model performance. However, the IID assumption, that variances associated with the component of a random utility expression describing each alternative are identical, imposes strong behavioural assumptions on the data. For this reason, alternative models have been proposed in the literature which may offer richer interpretations of the choice process.

The key alternative modelling specifications that have emerged in empirical choice modelling work are the nested logit, the multinomial probit and the random parameter or mixed logit models. Examples of random parameter or mixed logit studies include Revelt and Train (1998), Bhat (1997) and McFadden and Train (2000).

The mixed logit model may be interpreted as arising from taste heterogeneity in a population of MNL (McFadden and Train 2000). Train (2003) purports that the mixed logit model overcomes three limitations of standard logit by allowing for random taste variation, unrestricted substitution patterns and correlation in unobserved factors over time. More specifically, the mixed logit model can examine the proportion of the sample that have positive versus negative preferences. This is important if, over the sample, respondents are spread evenly over preference intensities. In this situation, the conditional logit model will provide an insignificant coefficient. McFadden and Train (2000) provide strong theoretical support for the mixed logit model type of approach for discrete choice problems. Nested logit models assume that some alternatives are nested under a category that is important to the respondent, and therefore needs to be estimated in the model.

3.1.2 The Outputs of Choice Models

Choice modelling provides two different types of value estimates. The first, known as implicit prices, are estimates of the value of a change in an environmental or social attribute. These are based on the marginal rate of substitution (MRS) between a cost or dollar value attribute and a non-monetary attribute. The second type of value estimates are compensating surpluses, which show respondents' willingness to pay for a bundle of changes. This may be different from the sum of the changes in the implicit prices if the value that respondents have for a bundle of changes is not simply the sum of the value of the individual changes. A significant advantage of the choice modelling approach is that it is possible to estimate the willingness of the respondent to pay for more of an environmental attribute. Through these measures the random utility model represented by the MNL function provides a means of assessing the effects of a wide range of policies through estimating changes in utility.

3.2 ELICITING SOCIAL WELFARE PREFERENCES: A RANDOM WELFARE MODEL

The measurements of compensating surpluses and implicit prices in many choice modelling studies are classified as welfare measurements. More precisely, though, they are estimates of changes in utility expressed in dollar terms. We explore a broader application of choice modelling by addressing the question of the distributional effects of policies and the consequent social welfare outcomes of policy alternatives. Rather than applying the random utility model to the estimation of utility and value in a dollar measure, the random utility model is applied to the estimation of the social welfare preferences of respondents, as illustrated in a social welfare function (SWF) and described in Chapter 2. The choice between the current distribution associated with the status quo and a change in policy that will result in distributional change is presented to respondents. The attributes of the policy options that are varied are the levels of utility of particular groups within society. In this instance, the MRS or 'implicit price' reflects the willingness of respondents to trade off a change in the utility of one group for a change in the utility of another group.

While the random utility model usually presents problems in the context of a private choice with individuals maximizing utility, in the context of social justice choices it is the maximization of social welfare that is relevant. It is assumed that respondents are able to make the distinction between day-to-day participation in the market economy, where decision-making is based on utility maximization, and participation in collective decision-making with the objective of maximizing social welfare. The social welfare theory introduced in Chapter 2 is based on the assumption that each individual has a personal set of social welfare preferences reflecting their notion of what they consider to be a fair distribution, and their individual perspective of social justice. These ethical judgements, embodied in every individual's SWF, are the foundation of the *random welfare model* to be developed.

Based on the theoretical foundations of the random utility model, there are two elements central to the model:

- a function that relates the probability of a distributional outcome to the welfare associated with each alternative; and,
- a function that relates the welfare of each alternative to a set of attributes which, together with estimated welfare parameters, determine the level of welfare of each alternative.

The decision rule is based on welfare maximization from a social justice point of view rather than an individual utility maximization perspective. Use of this decision rule further requires that the decision-makers are compensatory in their decisions; that is, willing to trade off the utility between groups.

In a similar vein to the random utility model, in the random welfare model it is assumed that welfare comprises two components: an observed welfare function and an unobserved component. Thus, the SWF of individual j for alternative q can be expressed as:

$$W_q^j = w_q^j + \varepsilon_{qj} \tag{3.5}$$

where W_q^j is the deterministic part of the welfare function and ε_{qj} the stochastic component. The error term acknowledges that it is difficult to describe welfare completely in terms of the utilities of groups and that there may be some groups who contribute to an individual's social welfare function but have not been included in the analysis. It also allows for the fact that there may be mistakes made in the measurement of the contribution of identified groups to the social welfare function.

It is assumed that the social welfare function (w) of respondent j is a linear function of the utility of groups $1...m$.

$$w_q^j = \beta_1 + \beta_2 v_{1q}^j + \beta_3 v_{2q}^j + ... + \beta_m v_{mq}^j \tag{3.6}$$

where the attribute v_{mq}^j is an estimate by the respondent j, of the utility to group

$1 \ldots m$ from the specific alternative q. The utility of group m is assumed to be a function not only of income but also of access to goods and services. In an environmental policy context, it is important to stress that utility may also be dependent on access to environmental goods and services.

When a respondent is asked to compare two alternatives in the choice model, it is assumed that the respondent is comparing the welfare he or she thinks society attains from each alternative and is then selecting the highest social welfare option. Hence, a key assumption of the random welfare model is that respondents are able to remove their personal self-interests and respond from the perspective of expressing their social justice preferences. The ability of respondents to view policy in this manner is supported in a study of the equity considerations of the burden of meeting the costs of environmental policy (Atkinson et al. 2000).[5] Strong support for the proposition that respondents significantly allowed their own position to influence their ranking of different options is not found in the literature. Consequently, a degree of interpersonally comparable cardinal utility is assumed. It is also assumed that respondents have some knowledge of the well-being of groups within society under the status quo policy.

The probability that any respondent (person j) prefers option g in the choice set to any alternative, option h, can be expressed as the probability that the welfare associated with option g exceeds that associated with all other options, that is:

$$P[(w_g^j + \varepsilon_{jg}) > (w_h^j + \varepsilon_{jh})] = P[(w_g^j - w_h^j) > (\varepsilon_{jh} - \varepsilon_{jg})] \qquad (3.7)$$

This indicates that respondent j will choose option g over option h if the difference in the deterministic parts of his/her welfare function exceeds the difference in the error parts. In order to derive an explicit expression for this probability, it is necessary to make an assumption about the distribution of the error terms (ε). Assuming they are independently and identically distributed (IID) and follow an extreme value type I distribution, the distribution can be expressed as:

$$P(\varepsilon_q \leq \varepsilon) = \exp(-\exp - \varepsilon) = e^{-e^{-\varepsilon}} \qquad (3.8)$$

From this foundation, the basic choice model can be applied within a welfare context. Assuming welfare maximization, the probability of any particular alternative q being chosen as the most preferred can be expressed as:

$$P_q^j = \frac{\exp(\delta W_q^j)}{\sum_{k=1}^{K} \exp(\delta W_k^j)} \qquad (3.9)$$

Remembering that W_q^j is assumed to be linear, additive functions in the attributes (in this case, utilities) which determine the welfare of the qth distribution, W_q^j can be written as:

$$W_q^j = \sum_{m=1}^{M} (\delta\beta_q^j) V_{mq}^j \qquad (3.10)$$

The welfare parameter β_q^j provides an estimate of the weight of group m in the welfare expression of alternative q, from the perspective of respondent, j. The scalar parameter within the random welfare model is represented by δ.

The mixed logit form of this model is developed in the same manner as with the random utility model – that is, by introducing into the welfare function through β_q additional stochastic elements that may be heteroskedastic and correlated across alternatives.

3.2.1 Relating the Random Welfare Model to the Distributional Weight

The key output of the random welfare-based choice model is the social marginal rate of substitution (SMRS), which is the ratio of the marginal welfare parameters:

$$SMRS_{q1m}^j = \frac{\delta\beta_{q1}^j}{\delta\beta_{qm}^j} = \frac{\beta_{q1}^j}{\beta_{qm}^j} \qquad (3.11)$$

that is, the willingness of respondent j to trade the utility or well-being of group 1 for the utility of group m given alternative q. By focusing on the ratio of the welfare parameters, the problem of the scale parameter is overcome. In effect, the SMRS reflects a willingness to accept distributional change, which can be represented graphically by the slope of the SWF, assuming a constant level of welfare. This distribution reflects respondent j's notion of social justice. Recall from Chapter 2 (Equation 2.19), that the distributional weight, when applied to a CBA setting, is a product of two components. These components are the change in social welfare if the utility of groups $1...m$ increases marginally, and the marginal utility of consumption of groups $1...m$. The SMRS estimated using choice modelling enables distributional weights to be estimated which incorporate these two components of the distributional weight.

3.2.2 Advantages in Using Choice Modelling to Estimate Welfare Changes

Freeman (1998) defines a social choice as a decision made by society to move to a certain social state. Even doing nothing is a social choice, as the alternative of doing something has been rejected. Social choice cannot be avoided. The use of choice modelling to address the distributional consequences of policy alternatives provides another means of eliciting the information required for informed social choice.

Two alternative forms of social choice procedure are voting on alternative social states or the delegation of authority to make social choices to a politically responsible agency, body or individual. In either case, it is valuable to know if choices actually reflect the underlying preferences or welfare functions of individuals. Yet, neither form of social choice procedure – voting or representation – can in principle determine social orderings and make social choices that conform to the preferences of individuals (Freeman 1998). Musgrave and Musgrave (1989) argue that the state as a cooperative venture among individuals must reflect their interests and concerns. Individuals do not live in isolation but are members of groups and thereby have common concerns. The application of a choice modelling approach to the question of social choice provides an alternative social choice mechanism. It provides the opportunity for social welfare orderings of the community at large to be voiced. An advantage of this approach is that it takes the value judgement away from policy-makers and economists and places it with the community.

Furthermore, in some environmental policy contexts, beneficiaries of various programmes and those with vested interests are more likely to be politically organized. They can thus influence political outcomes, whereas the interests of the unorganized general public are neglected (Persson and Tabellini 2000). Choice modelling can have a positive role in overcoming this potential policy bias. Finally, choice modelling is an appropriate preference elicitation method, as it characterizes the decision environment and is able to align itself closely with realistic policy options (Bockstael and McConnell 1999).

3.3 CONCLUSIONS

The literature introduced in Chapter 2 identified the need to explore innovative methods of estimating the social justice preferences of the community. The method of choice modelling has significant potential as a means of eliciting distributional preferences. The stated preference method of choice modelling is not without limitations, yet it is a rapidly developing research method with wide applicability to a number of research areas. In conventional applications, the theoretical foundation, based on random utility theory, results in the estimation of a utility function from which marginal values or implicit prices can be estimated. The broader application of applying it to the question of the distributional effects of policies and the consequent social welfare outcomes of policy alternatives provides the opportunity for the social justice preferences of the community to be elicited. The development of a random welfare model, where the emphasis is on the estimation of an SWF rather than a utility function, provides this framework. In this case, the measure of interest is the SMRS, or the willingness of respondents to trade the utility or well-being of one group for another. The estimation of an SWF and marginal welfare parameters provides a means of estimating distributional weights suitable for inclusion in a CBA setting.

The estimation of social welfare preferences is conditional on the assumption that respondents are able to make the distinction between decisions which maximize personal well-being and social justice choices. This assumption is not unrealistic, given the ability of members of the community to often readily express social justice preferences. The following chapter provides an example of one instance where a choice modelling study has been used to estimate the distributional preferences of the community. In this instance, the social justice question is that of distribution between generations and the frame for the choice model is the context of environmental policy.

NOTES

1. For more detail see, for example, Haab and McConnell (2002).
2. For further elaboration on contingent valuation, see Mitchell and Carson (1989) or Hanemann (2005).
3. Also known as Luce's Choice Axiom. See Luce (1959).
4. The essential difference between the extreme value type I and normal distributions is in the tails of the distribution. For the distributional form, see Hensher et al. (2005, p. 84).
5. Within the health economics literature, a study by Johansson-Stenman and Martinsson (2008) also illustrates the ability of respondents to express social justice preferences. In this case, the social justice issue is expenditure on safety-enhancing road investments that target different age groups and road user types.

4. Case study: design of intergenerational distribution choice experiment

4.0 INTRODUCTION

Having proposed the stated preference method of choice modelling as a means of estimating the distributional preferences of the community, this chapter outlines a case study which illustrates this innovative application of choice modelling. The case study addresses the specific distributional question of intergenerational equity.

The distributional preferences of the current generation with respect to future generations are an integral aspect of environmental policy decision-making. For example, the Stern Review on the Economics of Climate Change (Stern 2007, p. 23) suggests that:

> Questions of intra-and inter-generational equity are central. Climate change will have serious impacts within the lifetime of most of those alive today. Future generations will be even more strongly affected, yet they lack representation in present-day decisions.

The question of intergenerational distribution involves decisions about the balance between consumption by the current generation and consumption in the future. The resources available for future production and consumption are inherently dependent on the capital/consumption balance of the current generation.

The aims of this case study are twofold: first, to show that choice modelling provides a potential means for estimating social welfare preferences and, second, to estimate a set of intergenerational distributional weights suitable for inclusion in a cost–benefit setting for environmental policy decision-making. The first section of this chapter provides a review of the current literature with respect to the particular allocative question of intergenerational distribution. This literature briefly elaborates on theories of social justice within the context of justice between generations. As will be discussed, the question of intergenerational distribution is closely linked to the sustainability debate.

4.1 INTERGENERATIONAL DISTRIBUTION AND SUSTAINABILITY

Environmental policies affect the distribution of resources, both financial and environmental, between generations. Cost–benefit studies analysing changes to environmental policies often include benefits and costs which are borne by different generations. Hence, designing projects and programmes with the aim of equity within a single generation may be an inefficient way of serving the goal of distributional justice (Pearce 1993). As Sumaila and Walters (2005) emphasize, economists need to provide decision-makers with evaluation approaches that address legitimate policy questions such as intergenerational equity.

From a philosophical perspective, there has been widespread debate over the question of the current generation's responsibility to future people (Turner 1988). In his seminal work, *A Theory of Justice*, Rawls (1971, p. 284) asserts that the question of justice between generations subjects any ethical theory to 'severe if not impossible tests'. Solow (1986, p. 141) suggests that, at a popular level, discussion of intergenerational equity usually takes a simple form where the basic question is: 'how much of the world's – or a country's – endowment of non-renewable resources is it fair for the current generation to use up, and how much should be left for generations to come who have no active voice in contemporary decisions?'

The ethical debate regarding intergenerational equity can be related to the justice principles introduced in Chapter 2. For example, the well-known Ramsey (1928) model, which is concerned with optimal growth and capital accumulation, takes the sum over time of instantaneous utilities from consumption as its measure of social performance. This utilitarian ethic assumes that equity between generations is adequately taken care of by adding one generation's utility level to another's and treating each generation equally. Each generation's utility is assumed to depend only on its own consumption. As a consequence, the utilitarian ethic suggests that any generation should only sacrifice a unit of utility when this leads to an increase of more than one unit of utility for any other generation. Building on this early work, Attfield (1983) also advocated a variant of utilitarianism as the basis for a theory of normative ethics capable of providing a coherent treatment of obligations to future generations. Again, this required equal provision for the needs of each generation.

Rawls (1971, 2001) also addresses the question of how far the present generation is bound to respect the claims of its successors. Applying a Rawlsian criterion suggests that the justice principle be the standard of consumption achieved by the least well-off generation (Solow 1986). Rawls's principle of just savings is based on the notion that if society is to be a fair system of cooperation between generations over time, a principle governing savings is required, where savings may take various forms, such as manufactured capital and education. According to Rawls, this principle is one where the members of any generation would adopt the principle they would want preceding generations to have followed. Rawls emphasizes that saving is not required just to make future generations better off, but is a condition needed to bring about a just society (Tacconi 2000). In Rawls's theory, equity is expressed in terms of primary goods, which are regarded as things that every rational individual is assumed to desire. That applies not only to income and wealth, but also to rights, opportunities and the social basis for self-respect (Tacconi and Bennett 1995). Barry (1989) raises the point that the focus should not only be on the 'just' rate of capital accumulation, but also on the just rate of negative environmental factors, such as air and water pollution, degradation of the landscape and depletion of natural resources.

A further criticism of Rawls's theory with respect to intergenerational equity is a problem of circularity which is known as the 'Parfit Paradox'. Rawls outlines what is known as the 'original position' where a fair procedure leads to the adoption of principles that can be considered just. Rawls includes future generations in the original position. However, Parfit (1976, 1982) highlights the distinction between possible or potential people and future actual individuals who will exist at some subsequent time. Hence, the principles adopted in the original position may determine how many generations will exist and consequently how many generations will be represented in the original position.

Tacconi and Bennett (1995, p. 219) provide a constructive summary of the Rawlsian position with respect to the question of intergenerational distribution:

> A Rawlsian approach to intergenerational equity is useful in deriving general principles of justice and to decide on the potential resource patterns to be followed to achieve intergenerational equity. However, it cannot provide definitive answers to intergenerational resource distribution.

An alternative perspective to the problem that Toman (1994) describes as 'intergenerational fairness' is the development of arguments that invoke an obligation to the entire context of future human life; to the species as a whole and the ecological system rather than limited to potential future individuals (see, for example, Norton 1987). Toman (1994) suggests that this stewardship perspective does not deny the relevance of human preferences, but asserts the existence of larger societal concerns that members of society will feel (in varying degrees) beyond individualistic preferences.

Broome (1995) suggests a justice principle where we look for a class of reasons, referred to as 'claims', as to why one person should be given priority over another. He argues that fairness is about mediating the claims of different people and requires that claims should be satisfied in proportion to their strength. The important aspect of this view of equity is not simply how an individual fares in relation to his/her own claims, but also the relative extent of the claim and how he/she fares in relation to the rest of the claimants (Rescher 2002). In the context of intergenerational distribution, the claimants reflect varying generations and the question becomes one of weighing the gains and losses to different generations. An emphasis on the need to weigh up gains and losses between claimants is a feature of the choice modelling methodology.

In more recent times, intergenerational distributional issues are often raised under the banner of sustainability, as sustainable development implies some general rule about not impairing the capability of future generations to achieve the same level of well-being as the current generation (Pezzey 1989). The strong link between sustainability and social justice between generations has resulted in policy debates increasingly considering intergenerational distributional issues. Hanley et al. (2007, p. 14) suggest that 'economists would say sustainable development is indeed principally an equity rather than an efficiency issue'.

Common to all definitions of sustainability is the concern about the well-being of future generations (Krysiak and Krysiak 2006). For example, The Brundtland Commission (World Commission on Environment and Development 1987) defined sustainable development as 'development that meets the needs of the present without compromising the ability of future generations to meet their own needs' and Pearce and Barbier (2000) stress the 'fair treatment of future generations'. Stavins et al. (2002) elegantly define sustainability as dynamic efficiency plus intergenerational equity. Chichilnisky (1996) suggests that sustainability means the preferences of the current generation do not 'dominate' the preferences of future generations in determining intergenerational resource distributions. These definitions raise quantitative issues about the relative strength of preferences.

At the United Nations Conference on Environment and Development (UNCED) held in Rio de Janeiro in 1992, the Rio Declaration on Environment and Development was adopted. The declaration comprises 27 statements of principle for global sustainable development. The third of these principles is:

> The right to development must be fulfilled so as to equitably meet developmental and environmental needs of present and future generations. (UNCED 1993, p. 9)

These definitions highlight an anthropocentric policy focus that places emphasis on achieving a quality of life that can be maintained for future generations. However, it is impossible to know the exact conditions that will allow the certain existence of future generations. What equitably meeting the needs of future generations precisely entails is open to interpretation.

Tacconi and Bennett (1995) and Tacconi (2000) propose three degrees of intergenerational equity depending on the constraints on capital reduction.[1] They define extensive intergenerational equity as requiring equitable access to natural capital, intermediate intergenerational equity requiring only nonnegative changes in the stock of renewable natural capital[2] and minimal intergenerational equity requiring the maintenance of critical renewable natural capital that provides life-support functions.

Alternatively, rather than focussing on capital accumulation, Arrow et al. (2004) construe sustainability to mean that intertemporal social welfare must not decrease over time, thereby focusing on social welfare rather than maintenance of the economy's productive base. With an emphasis on social welfare, intergenerational utility distribution also depends on the social welfare preferences of current generations toward the utility of future generations. Arrow et al. (1996) argue that, although social welfare functions have been criticized for assuming interpersonal comparability of utility, there seems to be no way of addressing the ethical issues involved in making decisions affecting different generations without making some comparisons implicitly or explicitly about interpersonal comparability. Hediger (2000) further develops a social welfare based approach to sustainability by developing a 'sustainability-based social value function' which integrates principles of basic human needs and the integrity of the ecosystem and socio-cultural system.

To summarize, while sustainability and intergenerational equity are inter-related, sustainability on its own does not provide an irrefutable notion of intergenerational justice. As Krysiak and Krysiak (2006, p. 257) comment, sustainability is 'a minimal requirement for intergenerational justice and not a complete concept of justice in itself'. The literature suggests acknowledgement of the desire to consider the well-being of future generations in environmental policy decision-making. However, knowledge of how this desire translates more specifically into intergenerational distribution preferences is limited.

Overlapping generations' models have also been used to address the question of intertemporal efficiency and intergenerational fairness as criteria for social choice. Rawls (1971) rejects the notion that the way to handle the question of justice between generations is to propose that the current generation has obligations and duties to its immediate descendants. He argues that the aim of justice as fairness is to derive all duties and obligations from other conditions and puts forward the alternative of a motivational assumption. This stresses that the goodwill of parties stretches over two generations, with individuals having a desire to further the welfare of their nearest descendants.

The mechanism of 'the veil of ignorance' which Rawls applies (as indicated in Chapter 2) results in people not knowing their place within the distribution, let alone that of their descendants. Hence, positive preferences for the later generations may incorporate self-interest. Barry (1989) concludes that Rawls is 'probably right' in saying that the concern for the welfare of descendants extends only two generations or so, and that it starts 'running out pretty fast after that'. This raises the importance of the notion of overlapping generations.

Rawls believes that the interests of more remote generations will be taken care of so long as there are ties between successive generations.

The seminal paper of Howarth and Norgaard (1990) shows that the classic welfare theory results related to the effect of initial endowments on equity and efficiency can be translated from a static to an intergenerational setting. This model also brought the overlapping generations' analytical framework to the centre of sustainability research (Pezzey and Toman 2002). In a later paper, they further develop this concept by constructing a general equilibrium model with overlapping generations (Howarth and Norgaard 1992). The model shows that the valuation of non-market goods and social objectives are intertwined, leading to the conclusion that there is complementarity between economic values and social objectives.

The notion of positive preferences between overlapping generations is supported by the experimental findings of Johansson-Stenman et al. (2002) in a study involving students' preferences with respect to 'imaginary grandchildren' and future income distribution. They found that respondents were willing to trade-off 'non-negligible' amounts of money for increasing their grandchild's relative standing in society. However, as Collard (1978) points out, while it is likely that there are distributional preferences in favour of one's own children and grandchildren, the more interesting question is whether this positive ranking may be considered to extend to one's contemporaries and their heirs as well.

This brief overview of the intergenerational equity literature suggests that although there is widespread sentiment towards protecting the welfare of future generations, how this translates into policy assessment is vague. The use of choice modelling to estimate welfare preferences with respect to intergenerational equity provides an illustration of the potential of the application of choice modelling for quantifying social welfare preferences.

4.2 THE INTERGENERATIONAL EQUITY CHOICE EXPERIMENT

4.2.1 Identification of Attributes and Levels

Louviere et al. (2000, p. 122) highlight the need to understand the choice problem thoroughly, including gaining insights into how choices are made. They suggest that better models come from 'real understanding of the behaviour of interest and its antecedent links, which leads to significant insights into behaviour *before* parameter estimation'. Heeding this advice, the design for this research evolved from a wide-ranging process of consultation with colleagues, focus groups and seminar participants.

Figure 4.1, which is adapted from Hensher et al. (2005), provides an outline of the steps involved in designing a choice model. The explanation in this chapter of the design process of the intergenerational distribution choice modelling application broadly follows these stages.

The research design process

Stage 1: Problem refinement

Stage 2: Stimuli refinement

- Alternative identification

- Attribute identification

- Attribute level identification

Stage 3: Experimental design consideration

- Type of design

- Model specification

- Reducing experiment size

Stage 4: Generate experiment design

Stage 5: Allocate attributes to design columns

Stage 6: Generate choice sets

Stage 7: Randomize choice sets

Stage 8: Construct survey instrument

Source: Adapted from Hensher et al. (2005, p. 102).

Figure 4.1 The research design process

An important aspect of the design of a choice modelling application is the framing of questions to reflect appropriately the choices available to respondents. Technically, framing refers to 'the effects of the ways a situation is described or defined on ways in which people involve themselves with and experience that situation' (Blamey et al. 2001, p. 136). For this choice modelling application, the frame has two important aspects: the environmental policy context and the notion of making choices between policies which influence the distribution of well-being or utility between groups in society.

Choices which involve eliciting social welfare preferences require a degree of interpersonally comparable cardinal utility to be assumed, so that respondents are able to make judgements about the well-being of other groups in society. The interpersonal comparison of utility is not an unrealistic assumption, as people can be observed making comparisons between themselves and others. However, the real essence of the problem is trying to construct a universally agreed 'index' or measure of utility.

A difficulty with the problem refinement in this application lies with the two components of the distributional weight to be estimated. As previously outlined, the distributional weight is dependent on two components: how the respondent ranks a particular group or individual in their SWF and how the respondent assesses the value of a marginal change in consumption for the particular group or individual. The initial desire to segment the distributional weight into these two theoretical components added to the difficulties associated in designing this choice model. In the interests of pragmatism, it was decided to estimate the distributional weight without segmenting the components of the weight. This acknowledges the fact that, in determining social justice preferences, respondents inherently consider both the value of an extra unit to the receiving group and how the group ranks in their distributional preferences.

It is also assumed that respondents use their knowledge of the well-being of groups within society under the status quo policy in assessing policy changes. Choices between the distribution associated with the status quo and changes in policy resulting in distributional changes were presented to respondents. Therefore, decision-making was seen in a broader context of welfare maximization within a social structure rather than individuals maximizing their own utilities.

In focusing on community social welfare preferences the emphasis is on respondents. Nyborg (2000) formalizes the distinction between 'homo economicus', the individual maximizing personal well-being and a utility function, and 'homo politicus', the individual expressing his or her social justice preferences. Focus on the behaviour of 'homo politicus' allows for a sense of social justice that Musgrave and Musgrave (1989) argue is essential for the definition of a good society and the functioning of a democratic society. Broome (1995) describes this as a notion of communal good that is separate from the good of individuals.

The traditional assumption of a veil of ignorance which is often assumed in welfare maximization was not employed in the choice modelling application. Hence, each individual's personal view of social justice based on his or her distributional preferences was sought. This does not preclude individuals' own personal utility being part of their social welfare preferences.

A priority of the design was the desire to focus the attention of respondents on the distribution of utility or well-being, within the frame of intergenerational distribution in an environmental context. Importantly, it was necessary to attempt to distil distributional preferences from environmental preferences. For this reason, hypothetical policies with generic labels were used in an attempt to ensure that values other than equity preferences were not reflected in respondents' choices. The use of hypothetical examples also encouraged respondents to remove their own utility from the decision-making process and centre on their social justice preferences. This does not mean that they do not bring preconceived beliefs to the decision-making process, rather that these beliefs are part of ethical preferences regarding social welfare and not utility-maximizing preferences.

Given the cognitive difficulty of the choice modelling application, the number of policies which were presented in each choice set was limited to three, and generic labels, for example Policy A, Policy B, etc., were chosen. The choice modelling application was unlabelled in the sense that the names A and B do not convey meaning to the respondent about what the alternatives represent in reality, and do not provide any useful information to suggest that there are unobserved influences that are systematically different for alternatives A and B (Hensher et al. 2005).

Bennett and Adamowicz (2001) contend that an important element in behavioural choice tasks is providing the option for respondents not to choose any of the available alternatives. Similarly, Hensher et al. (2005) suggest that unrealistically forcing decision-makers to select among the available alternatives is likely to over-inflate any estimates obtained. Hence, as the choice presented is one where it is realistic to have the choice of not changing policy, this alternative was provided for respondents. In each case, the option of choosing Policy C, described as a 'no change' policy, was provided. In summary, each choice set was limited to a choice between three policy alternatives: two generically labelled policies and the 'no change' policy option.

Having determined the policy alternatives, the next decision in the design process was determining the attributes defining each policy option. In this experiment, the attributes describe the impact on the utilities of individuals from different generations of the three hypothetical and generic policy options. A number of issues required clarification in determining the attributes for the experiment. One of these was the number of generations to be included and the problem of the timing of the benefit or cost in the experiment. The final chosen design limited the choices to generations currently living to avoid time and discounting complications, acknowledging the trade-offs required when considering the cognitive demands placed on respondents. The total time period of the analysis could have been extended by increasing the number of attributes. However, this would also have increased the cognitive burden for respondents and there is likely to be a trade-off between the number of attributes and valid responses (Louviere et al. 2000).

Following Mackay (1997), a time span of 25 years was taken as a generation. Hence, the generations described by the attributes are those currently *aged 50*, those *aged 25* and those who are *newborn*. Opinions expressed by participants in the focus groups suggested that the general public would be comfortable with this definition for a generation and for making choices between these three generations.

In each aspect of the design the main objective was limiting the cognitive demands to be placed on respondents in eliciting information about a relatively difficult concept. Three attributes, describing currently living generations, provided a balance between the desire to investigate how attitudes changed as the time horizon lengthened and the practical need not to overstretch the difficulty of the questionnaire for respondents.

Determining a means for describing changes in utility was a challenge that was confronted in designing the research. After consultation with the focus groups' participants, it was decided to describe the levels of the attributes in dollar terms. The dollar terms were used to reflect the change in utility to the individual with the specific characteristic described by the attribute. Dollars were adopted as a metric with which respondents could associate. The main advantage with this numéraire is that dollars are a common metric. Furthermore, it is with dollars that governments work to redistribute wealth via the tax and social security systems.

The distributional weightings may be sensitive to the choice of numéraire and it is likely that if a different numéraire had been applied, the distributional weights would be different. Theoretically, a possible solution to this difficulty would be to describe the attributes in terms of an 'index of well-being'. This has been used to make a theoretical case in an example by Broome (1995) and in an empirical exercise by Cummins (2006). Although an index of well-being encourages respondents to think in terms of welfare being broader than dollars and therefore more in line with the notion of welfare in the literature (Sen 1982, 2000), the difficulty and subjectivity in determining an appropriate index, the values of components in the index and the descriptors of the index made it impractical in the design of this choice model. Even if these issues were resolved, the cognitive difficulty for respondents making complex decisions in an unfamiliar metric would remain a concern. For these reasons, dollars were adopted as the numéraire to describe the attributes; that is, the utility change to each generation.

The levels of the attributes involve the manipulation of attribute differences, not absolute values of the attributes. The hypothetical dollar values represent a one-off loss or gain to the people representing the group described by the specific characteristic determining the attribute. That is, it is marginal values of welfare which are of interest. Given evidence in the literature that preferences may be asymmetrical, it was also desirable to include both positive and negative changes in the levels of the attributes.

As a result, five levels for each attribute were determined, again reflecting the need to compromise between competing objectives. On the one hand, the higher the number of levels for each attribute, the larger the full factorial for the experiment with associated statistical design impacts. On the other hand, there was a need to provide sufficient levels to accommodate both losses and gains in utility. Balancing these objectives, it was decided to design the application around five levels.

The intervals between the levels was influenced by Blamey et al. (2001) who suggest that levels in choice models be chosen to be equally spaced in either original units or some transformed units such as logarithms of levels. Consequently, each level in this choice model is equally spaced and the levels vary well-being to the value of plus or minus $A500. Feedback from the focus groups suggested this degree of variation was large enough to be significant to respondents in determining a choice and not unrealistic in representing a one-off gain or loss. The final attributes and levels for the intergenerational distribution choice model are provided in Table 4.1.

Table 4.1 Attributes and levels in intergenerational distribution choice modelling application

Attribute	Levels ($A)				
Utility change person Aged 50	−$1000	−$500	+$500	+$1000	+$1500
Utility change person Aged 25	−$1000	−$500	+$500	+$1000	+$1500
Utility change Newborn	−$1000	−$500	+$500	+$1000	+$1500

4.2.2 Experimental Design

A factorial experiment where each treatment combination is applied to at least one experimental unit is called a complete factorial. With three attributes each described by five possible levels, the complete or full factorial for this choice model is 5^3 or 125 alternatives, and these are then combined to form choice sets which further increases the number of potential combinations. Hence, the total number of treatment combinations is too large to allow the use of a complete factorial experiment, thereby requiring a subset of the complete factorial – that is, a fractional factorial.[3] A fractional factorial is a selection of the available attribute level combinations derived from the full factorial (Bennett and Adamowicz 2001).

The design adopted for this choice modelling application was taken from Lazari and Anderson (1994), who present a number of choice experiment designs that enable estimation of both main effects and attribute cross-effects or interactions. Louviere et al. (2000, p. 86) define a main effect as 'the difference in the means of each level of a particular attribute and the overall or "grand mean", such that the differences sum to zero'. Although main effects are of primary interest in experimental design, the interaction effects are also of interest. An interaction between two attributes will occur if respondent preferences for levels of one attribute depend on the levels of a second.[4] Main effects typically account for 70 to 90 per cent of explained variance (Louviere et al. 2000).

The chosen design, which has been constructed from an orthogonal main effects design, is suitable for experiments with five or fewer attributes and five levels for each attribute. Historically, choice experiment designs have relied on orthogonal fractional factorial designs. However, more recently, there has been growing interest in statistical design theory (Hensher et al. 2005). Statistical design theory can be applied to optimize the efficiency of designs for choice models and Louviere (2006) emphasizes the importance of efficient designs. The design by Lazari and Anderson (1994), which has been adopted for the intergenerational distribution choice model, is a statistically efficient design.

Twenty-five choice sets were constructed from the experimental design. Each set comprised three choice options. The first choice option or policy alternative was the initial profile in the experimental design. The second choice options were determined by randomly sorting the treatment combinations. The random selection was achieved using Microsoft Excel to randomly allocate a value to each profile and then sorting the randomly allocated values numerically. The third choice option applied to each set was a status quo option which provided the 'no change' policy option.

One strategy used to cope with the large number of choice sets created, even with the use of a fractional factorial, is to segment the fractional factorial into blocks (Bennett and Adamowicz 2001). In this experiment, the 25 choice sets were segmented into five blocks, each consisting of five choice sets. Each respondent was therefore only exposed to the alternatives that comprise one block of the fractional factorial. The blocking strategy requires an assumption of identically distributed preferences across respondents (Bennett and Adamowicz 2001).

Bennett and Blamey (2001) recommend that once the choice sets have been created using the experimental design, it is important to review each set for the presence of implausible or dominated alternatives. They suggest that what constitutes a dominant alternative is usually far from clear cut. Consequently, the sets with apparent dominant alternatives were not removed from the choice sets in order to maintain the integrity of the experimental design. Maintaining the apparent dominant alternatives in choice sets also has the advantage of possibly providing an indication of the respondents' cognitive understanding of the decisions presented to them.

In summary, stages one to seven of the research design process outlined in Figure 4.1 were followed in order to generate the 25 choice sets to be used in the intergenerational distribution choice modelling application. The final stage of the design process was the construction of the research questionnaire.

4.2.3 Questionnaire

The design of the questionnaire was mindful that language in research settings often differs from language in everyday conversations (Svedsäter 2003). Hence the aim was to express the research questions in a manner with which people in the general community would be able to associate. The challenge was to convey to respondents the social justice preferences which were being elicited while avoiding the economics language of utility and social welfare. Respondents were encouraged to adopt this approach by the following introduction to the questionnaire:

> Many environmental policies result in a transfer of both income and resources between generations. For example, some environmental policies are paid for by current taxpayers with the aim of improving the environment for future generations. We are interested in finding out what you think about the way these policies lead to gains for some generations and costs for other generations.

The questionnaire was constructed with the aim of reminding respondents that the dollar values represent the general well-being of the individual, and should not be interpreted as financial wealth alone, as it was recognized that a disadvantage associated with this choice of numéraire is the difficulty for respondents to think in terms of general well-being or welfare and not simply income. As discussed, the main advantage with this numéraire is that dollars are a common and well understood decision-making metric for respondents. Respondents were advised in the following way that the dollar values represented the general utility of the individuals, and should not be interpreted as financial wealth alone:

> In this survey, dollars have been used to measure the gains and losses to different generations. The dollar amounts represent gains and losses from changes to access to environmental resources such as air, water, forests and beaches as well as monetary wealth.

As can be seen from Figure 4.2, 'smiley faces' were used to represent the gains and losses in the choice sets. Although dollars remained the numeric, this assisted respondents in focussing on the fact that the gains and losses were in total well-being and not just financial wealth. A bold line either above or below the smiley faces to represent gains and losses and the mouth of the face were also used to reinforce the distinction between gains and losses, with a smile for gains, a down-turned mouth for losses and a straight line for no change. The magnitude of the gain or loss was represented by the number of smiley faces with each 'face' representing an $A500 change in utility or well-being. The relationship between dollars and smiley faces was outlined for respondents in the reference key of the questionnaire. Possible confusion about discounting was addressed with the explanation that 'the dollar values are in today's dollars to make comparison easier'.

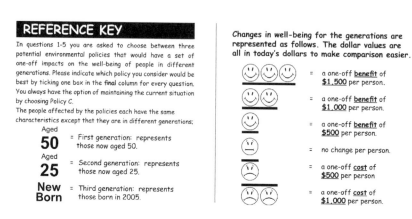

Figure 4.2 Reference key for choice sets

As the explanation in Figure 4.2 indicates, care was taken to indicate to respondents that the people receiving the gain or bearing the cost had the same characteristics except that they are in different generations. An example of the final choice sets incorporated in the questionnaire is provided in Figure 4.3.

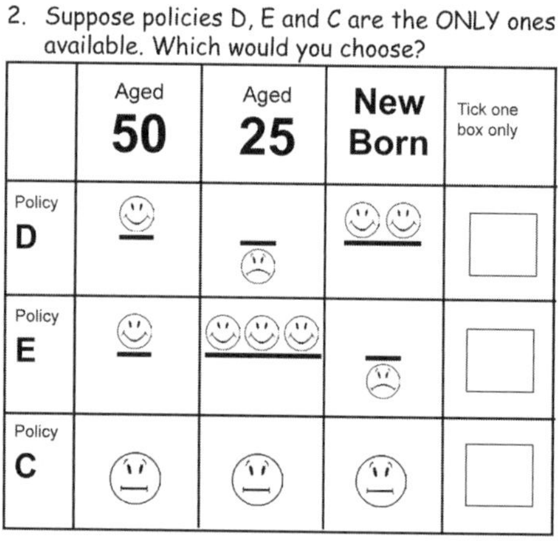

Figure 4.3 Example of an intergenerational utility distribution choice set

Encouragement to respond was provided by indicating to respondents the purpose of the survey in the following manner:

> By finding out how the community thinks about gains and losses to different generations caused by potential policies, environmental decision makers will be able to include community attitudes more accurately in their decisions.

Questions requesting socio-demographic details from respondents were also included in the research instrument in order to address the investigative question which suggests that distributional weights are sensitive to socio-demographic factors. These questions included general questions such as respondents' age, individual income, education level and gender. Although household income levels or household wealth may also be relevant in determining respondents' social welfare preferences, individual income was used to enable comparison with Australian Bureau of Statistics (ABS) (2001) Census data. Questions regarding parental status, number of children and grandparental status were also included in the socio-demographic questions.

Finally, two qualitative questions were included in the questionnaire: one asking respondents to outline briefly any particular strategy they used in making choices, and another seeking any further comments they wished to make about well-being across generations. This information was sought to gain further insight into the decision-making processes of respondents.

This chapter has provided some insight into the design process for a choice modelling application focusing on a distributional question. The are many aspects of this process which will require further development and research as the application of choice modelling to distributional questions progresses. The desire to elicit from respondents relatively complex information regarding social justice preferences results in a number of issues associated with the research design which require careful consideration. Foremost among these are decisions relating to the frame of the application and the necessary assumption regarding interpersonally comparable cardinal utility. The welfare economics literature assumes that people hold personal social welfare preferences. However, providing a means for respondents to articulate these preferences is challenging. The overriding consideration in this application was the need to minimize the cognitive burden being placed on respondents given the unfamiliar nature of the information being requested. A particular area of concern in the design was the decision to use money as the numéraire with which to express well-being. However, an attempt to minimize this difficulty was made by the use of graphic symbols, that is, smiley faces, to convey well-being. An integral aspect of the research design was the input from focus groups. The feedback from the groups provided valuable input into the research design and particularly the structure, language and layout of the final research questionnaire.

The focus groups indicated that once people understood what they were being asked, they were able to express clearly defined preferences. Hence, a priority in the construction of any questionnaire designed to elicit social welfare preferences is to convey to respondents, in everyday language, the desire to learn about their distributional preferences. The following chapter briefly discusses the results of this choice modelling application and the estimated intergenerational distributional weights.

NOTES

1. These relate to the distinction between 'weak' and 'strong' sustainability, with weak sustainability requiring the total capital stock to be non-declining and strong sustainability the natural capital stock to be non-declining.
2. This could imply that the stock of non-renewable natural capital is progressively depleted without consideration of the impact on future generations (Tacconi 2000).
3. For further detail on fractional factorial designs, see Dey and Mukerjee (1999) and Raktoe et al. (1981).
4. The availability cross-effects are a measure of the effect of the presence or absence of competing alternatives on the utility (or welfare in this case) of an existing alternative. If the IIA property holds, these effects will be zero. Thus the availability cross-effects are a measure of deviation from IIA. If two alternatives are very close substitutes for each other, the presence of the second (coded positive) may decrease the utility of the first more than expected by IIA and result in a negative availability cross-effect (Louviere et al. 2000).

5. Case study: results of intergenerational distribution choice experiment

5.0 INTRODUCTION

The *Environmental Choices Across Generations* questionnaire developed in Chapter 4 was used to conduct a household survey of a randomly selected sample of the general community using a personal drop-off and collection method. The results, which are summarized in Scarborough and Bennett (2008), are discussed here in further detail.

5.1 DATA COLLECTION

The sample was drawn from the community of Warrnambool, an Australian rural city in South-West Victoria with a population of approximately 35 000. A total of 503 households were approached, resulting in the delivery of 431 questionnaires. Of the 431 questionnaires which were distributed, 346 (80 per cent) were collected or returned by mail. This included 51 questionnaires (15 per cent of those collected) that were blank or significantly incomplete and consequently unusable. The remaining 295 were used for the data analysis, giving a usable response rate, from those distributed, of 68.5 per cent. For each of the 295 usable responses, five choice sets were completed. This resulted in a total of 1475 completed choice sets for analysis. When compared with the Australian census data, the socio-demographic profile of respondents indicated that those who are younger, female, and with higher income and education levels were likely to be more represented in the randomly selected sample.

5.2 DESCRIPTIVE STATISTICS

Table 5.1 summarizes the attributes and socio-demographic variables used in the intergenerational distribution choice model. The coding used to enter the socio-demographic data is also included.

The mean, standard deviation and number of observations for each variable are summarized in Table 5.2. The mean age of respondents based on the age categories rather than raw ages is 45 years. The mean income, based on income

Table 5.1 Variables used in the intergenerational distribution choice modelling application

Aged50	Change in the well-being of person representing those aged 50
Aged25	Change in the well-being of person representing those aged 25
Newborn	Change in the well-being of person representing those new-born
Age	Age of respondent in years (continuous variable)
Inc	Individual income of respondent in last year in thousands of Australian dollars (continuous variable)
Par	Parental status of respondent (0 = No, 1 = Yes)
Gpa	Grandparental status of respondent (0 = No, 1 = Yes)
Nos	If parent, number of children of respondent (1 = 1 child etc.)
Gender	Gender of respondent (0 = Male, 1 = Female)
Edu	Education level of respondent (Pre-secondary = −1, Secondary = 0, Post-secondary = 1)
Coll	Identity of person responsible for data collection (Recorded by initials of collector)

brackets, is $A36 000. Parental status was coded as 0 = No and 1 = Yes, hence the mean of 0.75 indicates that 75 per cent of respondents are parents. For those respondents who are parents, the mean number of children is two. As with parental status, grandparental status was coded 0 = No and 1 = Yes. The mean of 0.3 indicates that just less than one-third of respondents are grandparents. As gender was coded 0 = male and 1 = female, the mean of 0.59 reflects the slightly higher number of females in the sample. Finally, education was coded −1 = pre-secondary, 0 = secondary and 1 = post-secondary in terms of the highest level of education attained. Consequently, the mean of 0.14 indicates a mean level of education of respondents of slightly above secondary level.

Before proceeding with the statistical analysis, some general observations regarding the results of the experiment can be ascertained from an overview of the choice selections. One issue which this highlights is the selection of the status quo option. Samuelson and Zeckhauser (1988) have demonstrated the status quo bias and suggest that this effect is an implication of loss aversion where individuals have a strong tendency to remain at the status quo because the disadvantages of leaving it are perceived to be larger than the advantages. In this experiment, 12 per cent of respondents chose the status quo in each choice

Table 5.2 Descriptive statistics

	Mean	Std. Dev.	Number
Aged50	200	763.81	4425
Aged25	200	772.89	4425
Newborn	200	770.82	4425
Age	45.26	15.32	4365
Inc	36.50	20.23	4050
Par	0.75	0.43	4380
Nos	2.00	1.65	3720
Gpa	0.31	0.46	4380
Gender	0.59	0.49	4380
Edu	0.14	0.87	4365

set with which they were presented. The selection of the status quo policy alternative could reflect the possibility that respondents who were cognitively challenged by the choice sets selected the status quo. Alternatively, those who chose the status quo option (particularly over potential dominant profiles) may have been registering a form of protest vote where, because of objections to some aspect of the choice sets, they consistently selected the status quo without any consideration of the attribute levels being presented. This practice has been observed in other studies (see, for example, Burton et al. 2001).

It is difficult in this experiment to interpret the selection of the status quo option. In the experimental design, there are observations which are both above and below the zero implied in the status quo option. Although some respondents selected the status quo for all five choice sets presented to them, this cannot necessarily be interpreted as saying that these respondents were registering a form of protest vote in each case. The status quo may also have been a choice which in some cases represented, for example, a desire to see no cost borne by any generation. Furthermore, if respondents were concerned about the comparative changes in utility to the generations, the status quo option provided the most egalitarian policy with equal change (no change) for each generation.

A particular difficulty with the design of this experiment is that the status quo, or reference point, for each respondent is unknown. This will depend on the assessment by the respondent of the well-being of each group before any policy changes are introduced. The interpersonal cardinal comparability will be dependent on the respondent's individual social welfare function. Hence, the point on their social welfare function from which they are moving to make distributional change is unknown.

5.3 MODEL EQUATIONS

In the random welfare model introduced in Chapter 3 it was assumed that the social welfare function of respondent j, for alternative q, (W_q^j), is a linear function of the utility of groups $1\ldots m$, (v_{mq}^j). This equation is restated as Equation (5.1) in this chapter for convenience.

$$W_q^j = \beta_1 + \beta_2 v_{1q}^j + \beta_3 v_{2q}^j + \ldots + \beta_{m+1} v_{mq}^j \qquad (5.1)$$

Having now specified the design of the intergenerational distribution choice experiment, the social welfare function for each policy alternative can be expressed in terms of the specific attributes and socio-demographic characteristics. Thus:

$$W_A^j = ASC + \beta_{a50A} V(\cdot)_{a50A} + \beta_{a25A} V(\cdot)_{a25A} + \beta_{newA} V(\cdot)_{newA} + \beta_{A1} SDC^j + \beta_{A2} Coll \quad (5.2)$$

$$W_B^j = ASC + \beta_{a50B} V(\cdot)_{a50B} + \beta_{a25B} V(\cdot)_{a25B} + \beta_{newB} V(\cdot)_{newB} + \beta_{B1} SDC^j + \beta_{B2} Coll \quad (5.3)$$

$$W_C^j = ASC + \beta_{a50C} V(\cdot)_{a50C} + \beta_{a25C} V(\cdot)_{a25C} + \beta_{newC} V(\cdot)_{newC} \qquad (5.4)$$

where W_A^j refers to the welfare function of respondent j with respect to Policy A, and $V(\cdot)_{a50A}$ is the utility derived by those aged 50, from the level of environmental and consumption goods associated with Policy A, etc. The socio-demographic characteristics (SDC) of the respondents, including age, gender, parental status, number of children (if parental status is positive), grandparental status, income and education, are represented by SDC^j. A variable for the identity of the collector of the data (*Coll*) is also included in the model to test for any collector bias.

An ASC is included in the specification to estimate the change in utility associated with choosing an alternative other than the status quo alternative, Policy C. As Policies A and B are generic labels, the ASC for these alternatives is equivalent. It is the role of the ASC to take up any systematic variation in choices that cannot be explained by either the attributes or the socio-economic variables (Bennett and Blamey 2001).

In line with the social welfare literature outlined in Chapter 2, it is assumed that the decision rule for each respondent is welfare maximization. It is likely that the criteria used for welfare maximization will vary across respondents. The βs indicate marginal changes to welfare from a change in utility to a particular group. The key output of the intergenerational distribution choice model is the social marginal rate of substitution (SMRS). Given that the attributes of the choice model are the changes in utility accruing to particular groups, the SMRS is estimated by the ratio of the marginal welfare changes (βs). For example, the SMRS for Policy A, by respondent j, between those aged 50 and those aged 25 is:

$$SMRS^{j}_{A\frac{a50}{a25}} = \frac{\delta\beta^{j}_{Aa50}}{\delta\beta^{j}_{Aa25}} = \frac{\beta^{j}_{Aa50}}{\beta^{j}_{Aa25}} \tag{5.5}$$

The SMRS reflects a willingness to accept distributional change, which can be represented graphically by the slope of the social welfare function. This reflects the respondents' social welfare preferences. The SRMS also yields distributional weights applicable to a CBA setting. This is the measure of particular interest in this choice experiment.

5.4 MULTINOMIAL LOGIT MODEL RESULTS

The results of the maximum likelihood estimation of the multinomial logit model are shown in Table 5.3. The model was estimated using the Nlogit software program.

Table 5.3 Intergenerational utility distribution multinomial logit model results

Variable	Coefficient	Std error	z	$P>/z/$
Aged50	0.0003	0.0001	5.45	0.000***
Aged25	0.0005	0.0000	9.07	0.000***
Newborn	0.0006	0.0001	10.22	0.000***
Age	0.0148	0.0064	2.33	0.020**
Inc	0.0106	0.0035	3.01	0.002***
Par	−0.5633	0.2347	−2.40	0.016**
Nos	−0.0202	0.0635	−0.32	0.750
Gpa	0.2041	0.2112	0.97	0.334
Gender	−0.1498	0.1363	−1.10	0.272
Edu	0.0145	0.0846	0.17	0.864
Coll	0.0126	0.0490	0.26	0.796
ASC	0.1332	0.7917	1.68	0.092
Model Statistics				
Log-likelihood	−1130.85			
Pseudo R^2	0.301			

Note: **Significant at 5% level; ***Significant at 1% level.

To determine whether the overall model is statistically significant, comparison is made between the log likelihood (LL) function of the estimated choice model and the LL function of some other 'base model'. Hensher et al. (2005) indicate that, in most studies, the base model used for comparison is either:

i) the LL function of a model fitted independent of any information contained within the data, that is assuming equal shares among the alternatives, or
ii) the LL function of a model fitted using only information of the market shares as they exist within the data set.

Following the recommendation of Hensher et al. (2005) the second option of a base model based on the shares within the data has been used. Table 5.4 shows the calculation of the pseudo R^2 for the model. Comparison of the −2LL value of 979.20 with a χ^2 statistic with 11 degrees of freedom of 19.67 indicates that the null hypothesis that the specified model is no better than the base comparison model can be rejected. With an LL of −1132.37, the pseudo R^2 for the model is 0.30.[1] Hensher et al. (2005) suggest that a pseudo R^2 of 0.3 represents an R^2 of approximately 0.6 for the equivalent R^2 of a linear regression model and is a 'decent' model fit for a discrete choice model.

Table 5.4 Calculation of pseudo R^2 for multinomial logit model

Model	LL	Deg free	Deg Free diff	−2LL function	Chi critical	Pseudo R^2
Base model	−1620.45	1				0.30
Estimated model	−1132.37	12	11	979.20	19.68	

Source: Based on Hensher et al. (2005, p. 331 and p. 338).

The z statistics in Table 5.3 give the Wald statistics for the variables which are equivalent to the t-statistic taken at various levels of confidence. Assuming a 95 per cent confidence level, the critical Wald value is 1.96. If the absolute value of the Wald-test statistic given in the output is greater than the critical Wald value, the hypothesis that the parameter equals zero can be rejected and it can be concluded that the explanatory variable is statistically significant (Hensher et al. 2005).

The p-values in Table 5.3 provide the probability value for the Wald test values. The p-values are compared to a pre-determined confidence level as given by alpha which assuming a 95 per cent confidence level equals 0.05. Any p-values less than the determined level of alpha suggest that the parameter is not statistically equal to zero and that the explanatory variable is statistically significant. The Wald test and *p*-values will draw the same conclusion at the same level of confidence.

In the results reported in Table 5.3, each choice set attribute parameter is significant at the 1 per cent level and signed as expected *a priori*, indicating that the utility of each age group contributes positively to the social welfare functions of respondents. Of the socio-demographic characteristics, the income variable is significant at the 1 per cent level and the age and parental status variables are significant at the 5 per cent level. The other socio-demographic variables – grandparental status, gender, education and, for those who are parents, the number of children – are not statistically significant, indicating that these characteristics are not significant in determining respondents' intergenerational distribution preferences. The variable for identity of the data collection person is also not significant, indicating that this was not a determining factor in the model. Further analysis of the socio-demographic variables is provided in the results of the mixed logit model in section 5.5 below.

The key outputs from the multinomial logit model are the mean SMRS which represent the willingness of respondents to accept distributional change. Table 5.5 summarizes the 95 per cent confidence intervals for the SMRS for the multinomial logit model, both including and excluding the socio-demographic variables. The simulation methodology proposed by Krinsky and Robb (1986) using 1000 replications has been used to obtain the mean confidence intervals. This technique simulates the asymptotic distribution of the maximum likelihood estimator of the welfare measure by taking repeated draws from the multivariate distribution defined by the coefficient estimates and their associated covariance matrix (Hanley et al. 2001). These results indicate a distributional preference by respondents toward the younger generations with the ratio of the welfare parameters being greater than one for both the *Aged25* and *Newborn* attributes relative to the *Aged50* attribute. For the multinomial logit model, excluding the SDC, the estimated mean SMRS are: 2.28 between newborns and those aged 50, 1.50 between those aged 25 and those aged 50, and 1.54 between newborns and those aged 25. For the multinomial logit model, including the socio-demographic variables, the estimated mean SMRS results are similar: 2.23 between newborns and those aged 50, 1.63 between those aged 25 and those aged 50, and 1.37 between newborns and those aged 25. The plausibility, policy implications and limitations of these results are discussed later in this chapter.

5.5 MIXED LOGIT MODEL RESULTS

In Chapter 3 the assumptions underlying the multinomial logit were outlined. One of these assumptions is the IIA property which assumes that the ratio of probabilities between any two alternatives is unaffected by other alternatives

*Table 5.5 Multinomial logit model: estimated mean social marginal rates of substitution**

	Aged 25/ Aged 50	Newborn/ Aged 50	Newborn/ Aged 25
Model excluding socio-demographic variables	1.50 (0.97, 2.37)	2.28 (1.47, 3.74)	1.54 (1.12, 2.10)
Model including socio-demographic variables	1.63 (0.94, 3.76)	2.23 (1.25, 5.26)	1.37 (0.89, 2.14)

Note: * 95% confidence intervals estimated with the Krinsky–Robb (1986) method using 1000 replications.

in the choice set. To decide if the IIA property is satisfied, Hausman and McFadden (1984) proposed a specification test. The model is first estimated with all alternatives. The specification under the alternate hypothesis of IIA violation is the model with a smaller set of choices, estimated with a restricted set of alternatives and the same attributes. The set of observations is reduced to those in which one of the smaller sets of choices was made (Louviere et al. 2000).[2] The Hausman and McFadden test was conducted on the intergenerational distribution multinomial logit model and compliance was not confirmed. The inability to confirm that the IIA assumption held within the model indicates that the mixed logit model, where the assumption is relaxed, may improve the data analysis.

With the mixed logit model, individual heterogeneity is introduced into the welfare function through the β_z which are assumed to vary across the population, and are drawn from some distribution: $\beta_z \sim F(b, \Omega)$. Estimation involves identifying the most appropriate distribution parameters for the assumed functional form, as β_z can take on different distributional forms such as normal, log-normal, uniform or triangular. Hence, the unobserved parameters can be considered to have two elements: the mean of the distribution and the stochastic distribution around the mean (Greene et al. 2005).

The attributes were included as random variables and different distributions were used to estimate the models. Given the *a priori* expectation that each of the parameters for the attributes is positive, the lognormal distribution was not discounted as an option (Hensher et al. 2005). However, the lognormal distribution did not provide a good model fit compared with the normal distribution. Other distributions resulted in minimal differences in the goodness of fit measured by the log-likelihood. Accordingly, the results of the model estimation with a normal distribution for each of the random parameters are presented.

The random parameters assigned over the sampled population are obtained from repeated simulated draws. The number of draws and draw method must also be specified by the analyst. A number of intelligent draw methods are available and Bhat (2001) reports that using Halton intelligent draws may reduce the number of draws required. Intelligent draws methods are designed to reduce the possibility of drawing parameters from limited sections of a distribution (Hensher et al. 2005). The results presented are estimates made using the standard Halton sequence draw method offered in NLogit. The number of draws was also varied and the estimates presented are using 500 random draws. This number of draws secured a stable set of parameter estimates. The results of the multinomial logit model with each of the attributes included as a random variable are summarized in Table 5.6.

Table 5.6 Intergenerational utility distribution mixed logit model results

	Coefficient	Std. error	z	$P>/z/$
Random parameters				
Aged50	0.0004	0.0001	3.568	0.000***
Aged25	0.0007	0.0001	3.867	0.000***
Newborn	0.0010	0.0002	4.091	0.000***
Non-random parameters				
Age	0.0224	0.0091	2.44	0.015**
Inc	0.0147	0.0051	2.86	0.004***
Par	−0.7219	0.3210	−2.25	0.025**
Nos	−0.0313	0.0804	−0.39	0.697
Gpa	0.2818	0.2838	0.99	0.321
Gender	−0.2428	0.1848	−1.32	0.189
Edu	0.0255	0.1114	0.23	0.819
Coll	0.0231	0.6458	0.36	0.720
ASC	0.2745	0.1516	1.81	0.070
Standard deviations of random parameters				
Aged50			1.744	0.0811
Aged25			2.747	0.0060***
Newborn			1.891	0.0586
Model Statistics				
Log L	−1125.22			
Pseudo R^2	0.31			

Note: **Significant at 5% level; ***Significant at 1% level.

The overall fit of the mixed logit model is slightly superior to that of the multinomial logit with a LL closer to zero, and a pseudo R^2 of 0.31

The parameters for the attributes in the mixed logit model are all positive, significant at the 1 per cent level and similar to the results of the multinomial logit model. The dispersion of the *Aged50* and *Newborn* attributes are not significant, however the dispersion of the *Aged25* attribute is statistically significant at the 1 per cent level. This indicates significant heterogeneity in the preferences of respondents toward the *Aged25* attribute. The model was also estimated with only the *Aged25* attribute included as a random variable, however this did not improve the model fit with a pseudo R^2 also of 0.31.

The SMRS results for the mixed logit model are compared with the SMRS results of the multinomial logit model in Table 5.7. The mean SMRS for the mixed logit model have been calculated using unconditional parameter estimates as recommended by Hensher et al. (2005). For each of the ratios, the preference toward the younger generations is confirmed. For the mixed logit model the estimated mean SMRS are: 2.34 between newborns and those aged 50, 1.75 between those aged 25 and those aged 50, and 1.36 between newborns and those aged 25. The confidence intervals for the SMRS in the mixed logit model are greater when compared with the multinomial logit model, reflecting the greater variations in people's preferences.

Table 5.7 Comparison of multinomial logit and mixed logit social marginal rates of substitution

	Aged 25/Aged 50 Mean 95% CI	Newborn/Aged 50 Mean 95% CI	Newborn/Aged 25 Mean 95% CI
Multinomial logit model (inc SDC)	1.63 (0.94, 3.76)	2.23 (1.25, 5.26)	1.37 (0.89, 2.14)
Mixed logit model	1.75* (0.59, 4.71)	2.34* (1.00, 5.83)	1.36* (0.77, 2.67)

Note: *The mean SMRS are calculated using the unconditional parameter estimates; other SMRS are calculated using the Krinsky–Robb (1986) method.

A Poe et al. (2005) test was conducted to test the differences between the welfare parameters derived from the multinomial logit and mixed logit models. The results presented in Table 5.8 show that the differences are not statistically significant. If there is no difference between the models, then the expected difference between the models is zero, and the expected proportion of differences less than zero is 0.5. The one-tailed test is for values to be less than 0.05 or greater than 0.95. If this condition is met, it implies that significant differences exist. The results of less than 0.95 indicate that significant differences between the model estimates do not exist.

Table 5.8 Poe et al. test results for differences between welfare parameters estimated by multinomial logit and mixed logit models

Welfare parameters Multinominal logit-mixed logit > 0	
Aged 50	0.8501
Aged 25	0.9240
Newborn	0.9278

5.5.1 Interactions Between Attributes and Socio-demographics in the Mixed Logit Model

The influence of the socio-demographic characteristics of respondents on inter-generational distribution preferences has been further explored in the mixed logit model by interacting the socio-demographic variables with the attributes describing changes in utility to the specified age groups. The results, presented in Table 5.9, reveal some significant sources of preference heterogeneity. The standard deviation of the *Aged25* attribute is again significant at the 1 per cent level, confirming heterogeneity in the preferences of respondents towards this age group.

The interaction terms between the income variable and the *Aged50* and *Newborn* attributes are significant at the 1 per cent and 10 per cent levels respectively. This suggests that differences in the *Newborn* and the *Aged50* attributes may, in part, be explained by differences in the individual income levels of respondents. The positive sign of the *Newborn:income* interaction indicates that those on higher incomes tend to have increased preference for the well-being of the newborn age group. Conversely, the interaction term between the *Aged50* attribute and the income variable is negative. This suggests that those on higher individual incomes are less likely to favour the aged 50 age group in their social welfare preferences.

The interaction between the age socio-demographic variable and the *Aged25* and *Newborn* attributes are both negative and significant at the 1 per cent and 5 per cent levels respectively, suggesting that older respondents are less likely to favour the younger age groups.

The interaction term of the gender variable with the *Aged25* attribute is significant at the 5 per cent level. The positive sign for the *Aged25:gender*

Cost–benefit analysis and distributional preferences

Table 5.9 Mixed logit model: socio-demographic variables interacted with attributes

	Coefficient	Std error	z	$P>/z/$
Random parameters				
Aged50	0.0008	0.0003	2.678	0.0074***
Aged25	0.0013	0.0003	4.039	0.0001***
Newborn	0.0009	0.0004	2.523	0.0116**
Heterogeneity around the mean				
Aged 50:age	−0.71E−06	0.65E−05	−0.110	0.9125
Aged 50:inc	−0.10E−04	0.39E−05	−2.636	0.0084***
Aged50:edu	−0.74E−04	0.89E−04	−0.838	0.4020
Aged50:par	−0.14E−03	0.23E−03	−0.594	0.5526
Aged50:gender	−0.21E−03	0.15E−03	−1.403	0.1607
Aged50:gpa	0.13E−03	0.22E−03	−0.600	0.5512.
Aged50:nos	0.12E−03	0.67E−04	1.767	0.0772*
Aged50:coll	−0.66E−05	0.49E−04	0.134	0.8931
Aged25:age	−0.18E−04	0.64E−05	−2.807	0.0050***
Aged25:inc	−0.83E−06	0.38E−05	0.223	0.8239
Aged25:edu	−0.83E−04	0.93E−04	0.899	0.3684
Aged25:par	−0.36E−03	0.25E−03	−1.462	0.1436
Aged25:gender	0.33E−03	0.15E−03	2.264	0.0236**
Aged25:gpa	0.16E−03	0.22E−03	−0.732	0.4643
Aged25:nos	0.81E−04	0.63E−04	1.283	0.1997
Aged25:coll	0.95E−05	0.51E−04	0.188	0.8505
Newborn:age	−0.19E−04	0.81E−05	−2.331	0.0197**
Newborn:inc	0.83E−05	0.45E−05	1.848	0.0645*
Newborn:edu	−0.78E−04	0.11E−03	−0.736	0.4616
Newborn:par	0.24E−04	0.28E−03	0.082	0.9345
Newborn:gender	0.12E−03	0.16E−03	0.761	0.4466
Newborn:gpa	0.74E−04	0.26E−03	0.280	0.7794
Newborn:nos	0.12E−03	0.80e−04	1.494	0.1351
Newborn:coll	0.39E−04	0.62E−04	0.633	0.5269
Standard deviations of random parameters				
Aged50			1.524	0.1275
Aged25			2.586	0.0097***
Newborn			1.282	0.1999
Model statistics				
Log L	−1127.35			
Pseudo R^2	0.304			

Note: * Significant at 10% level; **Significant at 5% level; ***Significant and 1% level.

interaction suggests females in the sampled population were more likely to favour the aged 25 age group.

Finally, the interaction term between the *Aged50* attribute and the socio-demographic variable for the number of children (of those who are parents) is positive and significant at the 10 per cent level. This suggests that those respondents who have a larger number of children are more likely to favour the oldest of the three generations in their distributional preferences.

In summary, the results of the mixed logit model are similar to those of the multinomial logit model in that the estimated model is a good model fit. The estimated SMRS confirm the finding of the multinomial logit model – namely, that when aggregated, the respondent sample displays distributional preferences which favour the younger generations. Analysis of the mixed logit model results indicates significant heterogeneity in the preferences of respondents towards the age group represented by the *Aged25* attribute. The significant socio-demographic variables in the multinomial logit model are income, parental status and age. The influence of the socio-demographic variables in the model is more comprehensive in the mixed logit model. When analysis of the interaction terms between the socio-demographic variables and the attributes is undertaken, parental status is not a significant factor in the mixed logit model in terms of the interactions between parental status and each of the attributes. However, the sign of the interaction does change from negative for the older generations to positive for the newborns, thereby possibly accounting for the significance of the variable in the multinomial logit model. The significance of a respondent's individual income in influencing distributional preferences is confirmed in both the multinomial logit model and the mixed logit model. In particular, the negative and significant interaction term between income and the aged 50 age group indicates that, of the respondent sample, those with higher incomes are less likely to favour positive utility changes to the older age group. The significance of the age socio-demographic variable is also confirmed with negative and significant relationships between age and the attributes describing the two younger generations.

5.5.2 Asymmetry of Preferences

A final area of interest in this data set is the treatment of gains and losses in utility by respondents. Research suggests that individuals value gains and losses differently (Kahneman and Tversky 1979; Kahneman et al. 2000). The descriptive statistics in Table 5.10 provide an initial picture of respondents' selection of each of the attributes with negative or positive levels of utility changes. The percentages show the number of times the attribute at the negative/positive levels were selected as a percentage of the number of times the attribute appeared with negative/positive levels in the experimental design.

Table 5.10 Percentage of choices by negative/positive levels for each attribute

Level of change	Newborn	Aged25	Aged50	Total
Negative	22.2	23.8	26.0	24.1
Positive	39.9	38.9	37.0	38.6

As expected, the total figures indicate that gains (positive levels of utility changes) were selected more frequently than losses (negative levels of utility changes). Consistent with the findings of the multinomial logit model and the mixed logit model, the figures also suggest that respondents were more likely to avoid negative utility changes to the newborns and more likely to favour positive gains to the newborns. Similarly, the percentage of gains that would have been attributed by the hypothetical policy choices to the aged 50 age group was below the average and the losses above the average. Hence, the descriptive statistics suggest that the treatment of gains and losses may have varied with the attribute or generation.

The influence of asymmetric preferences on respondents' choice strategies was further explored using the mixed logit model. Differences in the treatment of gains and losses for each of the attributes were analysed by splitting the variables, with levels equal to or above zero regarded as positive and levels below zero defined as negative. The results of the mixed logit with the split attributes are presented in Table 5.11. The negative change variables for each of the attributes are significant and the positive change variables are not significant. For the newborn and the aged 50 age groups the variables are significant at the 5 per cent level and for the aged 25 age group the negative change variable is significant at the 1 per cent level.

Table 5.11 Asymmetry of preferences

	Coeff	$P>/z/$
Aged50: Positive	0.0002	0.6665
Aged50: Negative	0.0036	0.0536**
Aged25: Positive	0.0006	0.1251
Aged25: Negative	0.0036	0.0943*
Newborn: Positive	0.0006	0.3374
Newborn: Negative	0.0041	0.0241**

Note: **Significant at 5% level; *significant at the 1% level.

The significance of the negative split of the attributes indicates differences in the treatment of gains and losses by respondents. The standard deviations for the aged 50 negative variable and the aged 25 positive variables were also significant at the 5 per cent level, indicating significant heterogeneity in the preferences of respondents towards these variables. The log-likelihood for the mixed logit model estimated with the split attributes was −1304, which did not improve the overall model fit given the increased degrees of freedom in the model.

The asymmetry of respondent preferences is further explored by examining each attribute level separately. The coefficients of the mixed logit model with the attribute levels effects coded separately are summarized in Table 5.12. The coefficients for the attribute levels highlight, in particular, the aversion of respondents to the highest level of loss in utility to the newborn age group. For newborns, the difference in the coefficient for a loss in utility to the level of $A1000 compared with a loss of $A500 is almost double, while for the aged 50 and aged 25 groups this difference in coefficients between levels of loss was not evidenced.

Table 5.12 Multinomial logit model with attribute levels coded separately

	Coefficient for attribute levels				
Attribute	−1000	−500	+500	+1000	+1500
Aged 50	−0.80***	−0.71***	−0.30***	−0.20**	Not sig
Aged 25	−0.78***	−0.87***	−0.30***	Not sig	Not sig
Newborn	−1.34***	−0.67***	Not sig	Not sig	Not sig

Note: *** Significant at 1% level; ** Significant at the 5% level.

In summary, the data analysis suggests an aversion by the respondent sample to the imposition of losses in utility to each of the age groups described by the attributes in the choice model. This aversion is strongest with respect to the youngest of the age groups, described by the newborn attribute.

5.6 DECISION-MAKING STRATEGIES

Hanley et al. (2001) contend that one problem associated with choice modelling is that, in the presence of complex choices, respondents use heuristics or rules of thumb to simplify the decision-making task. Some heuristics associated with difficult choice sets include maximin and maximax strategies and lexicographic orderings (Hanley et al. 2001). This section briefly discusses the qualitative analysis of the heuristics employed by respondents in determining their intergenerational distribution preferences. Further quantitative analysis of the decision-making processes of respondents is developed in Scarborough et al. (2009).

As discussed in Chapter 2, the social welfare literature suggests that individuals may apply identifiable principles in determining their distributional preferences. Louviere (2006, p. 180) argues that 'it is not possible to learn about decision rules unless complete factorials or all possible choice sets' are used. This limitation is recognized, however some observations based on the qualitative data extrapolated from the research questionnaire can be made.

In the intergenerational distribution choice modelling application, respondents were provided with the opportunity to answer a qualitative question regarding the decision-making strategy they employed in determining their choices. Of the 295 respondents to the questionnaire, 114 chose to explain the strategy they applied in answering the choice questions. The responses indicate that, in general, those who chose to elaborate on their decision-making strategy appeared to have a clear understanding of the preferences that the questionnaire was seeking to elicit. A number of decision-making strategies can be identified.

The preference towards the utility of younger generations evident in the quantitative analysis is one decision-making strategy which is supported by the comments made by respondents to the qualitative questions regarding the strategy they used to make choices. Examples of these comments include:

> 'Help younger generation and early workforce people.'
> 'Picked ones that were most likely beneficial to the younger generation.'
> 'Thinking about effect on future generations.'

This decision-making strategy of maximizing the group which the respondent appears to consider the least well-off group broadly follows a Rawlsian strategy. The group which was commonly considered by respondents to be the least well-off was the youngest generation, hence this strategy appeared to be employed in a desire to both maximize the gains and minimize the costs to the youngest generation. A Rawlsian strategy may also have been evident with either of the other age groups identified as the least well-off group. However, this is not evident from the qualitative data.

Another decision-making strategy observed in the qualitative comments is a utilitarian approach, where the respondent's choice was based on a desire to maximize the total gain to all groups; that is, the sum of the smiley faces in the questionnaire. Comments that suggest this strategy include:

> 'Picked the policies that would benefit the most groups.'
> 'Most better off.'
> 'Benefits the most amount of people.'
> 'The more smiley faces the better.'

The extent to which respondents adopted a utilitarian approach was also investigated by creating a dummy variable for the total utility change of each alternative. When tested, the variable for the total was not statistically significant in the multinomial logit model. However, Table 5.13 compares the correlation between this variable and the choice variable with the correlations of each of the attributes and choice. The higher correlation between the total and the choice variable supports the qualitative analysis that some respondents adopted a utilitarian decision-making strategy.[3]

Table 5.13 Correlation between choice variable and both individual and sum of attributes

	Aged50	Aged25	Newborn	Total
Correlation with choice	0.0866	0.1289	0.1402	0.1996

An egalitarian approach was also evident as a decision-making strategy. Comments which support this view include:

'Fairest option for all age groups.'
'Fairness.'
'A balance should be attempted.'

As discussed, it is also possible that an egalitarian strategy contributed in some cases to the decision of those who chose the no-change policy option. In this instance, where the status quo was maintained, all groups received an equal outcome.

A final decision-making strategy evident in the qualitative analysis is that of self-interest. This is reflected in comments such as:

'Least cost to me.'
'Most beneficial to myself.'
'What would benefit me the most.'

When these comments are viewed in conjunction with the quantitative results, the extent of self-interest is difficult to determine. The interaction between the *Aged50* attribute and age is not statistically significant. However, the interactions between age and both the *Aged25* and *Newborn* attributes are negative and statistically significant. This suggests that, of the respondents, those who are older are less likely to favour the younger generations in their utility distribution preferences. This possibly reflects a degree of self-interest.

Although the evidence regarding the heuristics used by respondents is qualitative and inconclusive, it nevertheless suggests that a number of respondents employed identifiable decision-making strategies in determining their social welfare preferences. More than one-third of respondents were able to express the strategies they adopted in determining distributional preferences reasonably and succinctly. The identified strategies reflected a number of distributional principles identified in the social welfare literature.

5.7 POLICY IMPLICATIONS OF INTERGENERATIONAL DISTRIBUTION CHOICE EXPERIMENT

The policy implications of these results, suggesting positive preferences by respondents toward the younger generations, are significant for the development of environmental policy. The distributional weight of approximately 2.3 between those aged 50 and newborns suggests that, for the intergenerational equity preferences of the respondent sample to be incorporated in a CBA, benefits accruing to the newborn generation could be multiplied by 2.3. Using the example from Table 2.2 in Chapter 2, and assuming gains or losses only to the newborn age group, Table 5.14 illustrates the application of these findings to the hypothetical CBA setting. In Panel A, when no distributional weights are applied, the results of the CBA suggest that the project be accepted. However, the incorporation of intergenerational equity preferences, as illustrated in Panel B, indicates that the project should be rejected.

Table 5.14 Applying intergenerational equity distributional weights in CBA

Panel A: Comparison of unweighted gains and losses			
	Gain	Loss	Net gain
Those aged 50	+10	−4	+6
Newborns	+2	−6	−4
Aggregate gain	+12	−10	+2

Panel B: Comparison of weighted gains and losses*			
	Gain	Loss	Net gain
Those aged 50	+10	−4	+6
Newborns	+2 × 2.3 = +4.6	−6 × 2.3 = −13.8	−9.2
Aggregate gain	+14.6	−17.8	−3.2

Note: * In this hypothetical example, the gains and losses have been weighted equally to avoid complication.

This hypothetical example illustrates the potential impact of incorporating equity preferences in CBA. However, it also initiates subsequent discussion regarding the efficacy, complications and limitations of incorporating distribution in decision-making. This discussion is developed in Chapter 6.

This study provides one estimate of community preferences regarding intergenerational equity and highlights the need for further research regarding the distribution of resources between generations. The magnitude of the positive weighting toward the utility of future generations reported in the results of this choice modelling application supports the contention of Arrow et al. (2004) that individuals derive a positive externality from the welfare of future generations. Although undertaken in this instance within the context of environmental policy, the issue is also relevant for other policy areas, particularly fiscal policy.

5.7.1 Intergenerational Equity and the Social Discount Rate

As discussed in Chapter 4, the policy implications of incorporating intergenerational equity preferences in cost–benefit studies assessing environmental and natural resource management policies are particularly relevant in terms of the sustainability debate. A central aspect of this debate is the trade-off between consumption today and consumption in the future. The intertemporal problem of justice differs from the contemporary in that the resources are productive, so a transfer from an earlier to a later generation means, in general, that the later generation receives more.

Hence, a final policy implication of the estimated intergenerational distribution weights is the nexus between intergenerational equity and the social discount rate. Economic theory suggests that in order to incorporate intertemporal changes into a decision-making framework, the future benefits and costs should be discounted and compared in present value terms. High discount rates may result in decisions that make inadequate provisions for future generations. Conversely, failure to discount can also adversely impact the well-being of future generations.

In a social policy context, the intergenerational equity-adjusted present value of benefits and costs is the discounted future value multiplied by the intergenerational distributional weight:

$$PV = \alpha * \frac{1}{(1 + r)^t} * FV \qquad (5.6)$$

where α is the intergenerational distributional weight, r the social discount rate, PV the intergenerational equity-adjusted present value and FV the future value.

For example, without the application of distributional weights, a project with a current cost of $A100 and a future benefit in 25 years' time of $A200 would not be feasible in net present value terms with a 5 per cent discount rate (NPV of benefit is $A75). However, with the application of a distributional weight of 1.4 on the future benefits accruing to those in one future generation, the equity adjusted net present value is $A105 (and with a distributional weight of 1.6 is $A120) and the project becomes feasible.

Table 5.15 compares intergenerational equity-adjusted social discount rates derived from the application of intergenerational distributional weights with unadjusted social discount rates. This analysis is further developed in Scarborough (2011). The intergenerational equity-adjusted social discount rates have been derived by multiplying relevant discount factors by intergenerational distributional weights. The adjusted discount factors have been reported in terms of the corresponding discount rate. This decomposition of social discount rates illustrates that, for example, the application of a 1.4 per cent social discount rate in Garnaut (2008) could be interpreted as a 3 per cent social discount rate with the application of a distributional weight of 2.2 positively favouring benefits occurring two generations or 50 years in the future. Although these estimates simplify the complexities of discounting over different time horizons, they illustrate how decomposing the discount rate is important in understanding and estimating discount rates.

This explicit approach to incorporating intergenerational equity in policy analysis increases the transparency of analysis and decision-making and enables the segmentation of efficiency and equity criteria. While in Table 5.15 the weights estimated in this case study have been used as an example, this approach can also be used to explore the sensitivity of the social discount rate to assumptions with respect to the magnitude of the intergenerational distributional weights.

The segmentation of the efficiency and equity components of the social discount rate also raises a myriad of issues. In particular it highlights the potential trade-off between potential equity and efficiency considerations in decisions regarding the choice of social discount rate. This relates to the criticism of distributional weighting by Harberger (1978, 1984) and discussed in Chapter 2. Lower social discount rates may lead to the acceptance of policy alternatives which do not maximize efficiency and the size of the total 'pie' which is passed on to future generations.

From a policy perspective, the potential incorporation of intergenerational equity distributional preferences in policy analysis possibly strengthens the argument for adopting the opportunity cost of capital approach to estimating the social discount rate (Randall 2006). An adjustment for intergenerational equity applied to a capital-based social discount rate would circumvent possible double-counting of time preferences and intertemporal marginal

Table 5.15 Examples of intergenerational equity-adjusted social discount rates

Discount rate (%)	Number of years	Discount factor (df)	Distribu- tion weight (DW)	Adjusted discount factor (Adf)[a]	Equity-adjusted discount rate (%) (Ar)[b]
3	25	0.4776	1.4	0.6686	1.6
5	25	0.2953	1.4	0.4134	3.6
7	25	0.1843	1.4	0.2580	5.6
3	25	0.4776	1.6	0.7642	1.1
5	25	0.2953	1.6	0.4725	3.0
7	25	0.1843	1.6	0.2948	5.0
3	50	0.2281	2.2	0.5018	1.4
5	50	0.0872	2.2	0.1918	3.3
7	50	0.0339	2.2	0.0745	5.3

Notes: [a] $Adf = df * DW$

$$^{b} Ar = \frac{\ln(df)}{t}$$

utilities associated with incorporating intergenerational equity adjustments into a consumption-based social discount rate.

A further complication is the approach to uncertainty. Pannell and Schilizzi (2006) suggest that the resolution of issues concerning the social discount rate requires integration of efficiency, equity and uncertainty. Although further research is required, the role of uncertainty in the estimation of the social discount rate may increase over longer time horizons, while the adjustment for intergenerational equity may decline as the horizon extends. It is possible that the extent of positive intergenerational equity preferences towards future generations may decline after two generations in line with the decrease in genetic footprints.

5.8 CONCLUSION

There are two important considerations resulting from this case study. First, with respect to the specific distributional question of intergenerational equity, the results of this study suggest benevolence toward younger generations. In terms of distribution between generations, the findings indicate distributional preferences which positively favour the younger generations when making choices between currently living generations. The estimated SMRS of approximately 2.3 between two generations and approximately 1.4 over one generation show a willingness to trade losses in utility to the older generations for gains in utility to the younger generations when assessing the impact of hypothetical environmental policies. This study is not without its limitations. For example, the findings may be sensitive to the time horizon, particularly regarding preferences towards generations not currently living. Nevertheless, the results highlight the need for further research regarding the intergenerational distribution preferences of the community, as this is an integral aspect of environmental and natural resource management policy analysis.

Second, the results of the intergenerational distribution choice modelling application illustrate that respondents hold distributional preferences which can be elicited. The results indicate that the majority of respondents were able to understand the information which was being sought and to respond in a meaningful and considered manner to both quantitative and qualitative questions. This presents significant opportunities for further research aimed at improving the integration of equity in policy analysis. Chapter 6 discusses in more detail some of the challenges and opportunities associated with the application of choice modelling to the estimation of social welfare preferences.

NOTES

1. The pseudo R^2 is $1 - \dfrac{LL_{Estimated}}{LL_{Base}}$

2. For details of the test statistics, see Louviere et al. (2000, p. 161).
3. This needs to be qualified by the fact that the linear model will tend to reward choices that are high across the board.

6.   Choice modelling and distributional preferences: challenges and opportunities

6.0 INTRODUCTION

The case study presented in Chapters 4 and 5 has shown that choice modelling has the potential to be applied as a method for eliciting distributional preferences. This finding has important implications for the refinement of CBA as a decision-making tool both in environmental contexts and the broader policy sense. The policy implications of the results are in terms of intergenerational equity and the application of distributional weights in CBA. They raise a number of contentious issues which are discussed in this chapter. The subsequent discussion surrounds the efficacy, complications and limitations of incorporating distribution in decision-making. Hence, this chapter focuses on the challenges and opportunities associated with the application of the stated preference technique of choice modelling to the estimation of distributional preferences. The need for further research to enhance our understanding of distributional preferences is also addressed. The findings suggest many interesting, challenging and exciting potential developments for further research.

6.1 DISTRIBUTION AND CBA

Even if distributional preferences can be estimated, three central questions remain about the application of distributional weights in CBA. First, there is the appropriateness of including equity considerations in CBA, particularly given the inherent efficiency cost. Second, there is a problem about the aggregation of social welfare preferences, given that this requires a decision about whose social welfare preferences should be incorporated in an analysis. And third, determining the characteristic, or combination of characteristics, of the population upon which distributional preferences are to be estimated must also be addressed. Although income distribution is often an initial consideration in many policy settings, socio-demographic characteristics such as race, geography or generation may also be important when incorporating equity considerations in policy analysis.

With respect to the first question about the trade-off between equity and efficiency, some authors (as discussed in Chapter 2) argue that the specific policy level is not the most effective means to achieve distributional goals and that redistribution would be better achieved through other measures, such as through the fiscal system. For example, Kaplow (1996) and Ng (2000a,b) argue that distributional weights should not be applied, largely because of efficiency losses, and that the taxation system should be used to address equity issues.

Pearce (2006) focus on the cost of alternative measures of addressing distributional concerns. As the cost of the distributional transfers is important in the efficiency/equity trade-off, the debate becomes one about whether the taxation system is the most cost-effective means to implement distributional transfers or whether public-sector projects are also an efficient means for achieving some equity goals. This depends to some degree on the extent of the development of the tax and welfare systems. In some circumstances in less developed countries, the only acceptable method of making transfers may be via public-sector projects to provide social infrastructure such as schools and hospitals, or economic infrastructure such as roads and irrigation facilities. Drèze (1998) asserts that it is wishful thinking to assume that distributional concerns can be dealt with adequately through taxes, transfers and related policy instruments.

One limitation of this debate is the focus on income distribution when the range of distributional issues, particularly those associated with environmental policy, is much broader than income. This is illustrated by the wide range of environmental policy distributional issues discussed in Serret and Johnstone (2006). They argue that while environmental policy should not generally be the tool for addressing distributional issues, there are instances where, particularly for political reasons, the distribution of costs and benefits needs to be addressed within the context of environmental policy. Examples include the distribution of environmental quality or the distribution of exposure to pollution or environmental risk. In their view, 'the concept of fairness applied can have fundamental implications for the nature of interventions undertaken by public authorities' (Serret and Johnstone 2006, p. 6).

Randall (2002) suggests that most moral codes would imply paying some attention to individual preferences in social decision-making. Some economists focus on CBA as a useful decision-making tool which addresses the efficient allocation of resources. However, incorporating equity in CBA also needs to become an integral part of the decision-making process. It may be that, in the end, the distributional implications feed in to fiscal policy; however, the assessment of the distributional impact of policy change is nevertheless important.

The case remains, as Johansson (1998, p. 489) remarks, that 'one faces a formidable problem in assessing the social profitability of a project which affects more than a single person'. There is no doubt that the incorporation of distributional considerations in CBA makes the cost–benefit practitioner's task more difficult. Nevertheless, CBA is an important analytical tool for decision-makers. Furthermore, with distributional weights estimated, the CBA can be done in such a way that it either includes or excludes the weights in order to analyse the sensitivity of the results to their incorporation (Loomis 2011).

The potential to incorporate equity considerations in the decision-making calculus strengthens the potential of CBA as a tool for decision-making. There is also an increasing need for policy-makers to address distributional issues, as this can influence community acceptance of policy. The political acceptability of policy interventions may be enhanced by incorporating sensitivity to the gainers and losers in policy analysis. Furthermore, possible community dissatisfaction with environmental policy alternatives which are seen not to incorporate equity considerations also involves an inherent efficiency cost.

The second fundamental question with respect to incorporating equity in policy analysis is the question of whose preferences should be included. Concepts of justice may vary between actors who are in a position to influence the selection of specific procedures or criteria to allocate scarce resources. These actors include four main groups: individuals who are in the institution that is charged with the allocative task, political actors, claimants and public opinion (Elster 1992). Hence, notions of social justice will most likely vary between groups. While acknowledging that distributional preferences may vary depending on the role of different groups within society, more research is needed to explore the convergence or divergence in equity preferences between the groups delineated by Elster.

The findings of our reported case study support the contention of Arrow (1984, p. 66) that

> the individual plays a central role in social choice as the judge of alternative social actions according to his own standards. We presume that each individual has some way of ranking social actions according to his preferences for their consequences. These preferences constitute his value system. They are assumed to reflect already in full measure altruistic or egoistic motivations, as the case may be.

A distinct advantage of a choice modelling approach to estimating distributional preferences is the potential to enable respondents to express their personal social justice preferences. Arrow (1963) suggests that people have two distinct personalities: their self-interested selves who are essentially disjoint from their ethical selves. Self-interested preferences guide day-to-day participation in the market economy while ethical ones apply to participation in collective decision-making. Nyborg (2000) formalizes this distinction between 'Homo economicus', the individual maximizing utility, and 'Homo politicus', the individual maximizing his/her social welfare function. Focus on the behaviour of 'Homo politicus' allows for a sense of social justice which Musgrave and Musgrave (1989) argue is essential for the definition of a good society and the functioning of a democratic society. Broome (1995) describes this as a notion of communal good that is separate from the good of individuals.[1]

There is a degree of contention associated with assuming that respondents are able to make this distinction when determining their policy preferences. Are respondents able to express distributional preferences in a broader context of social structure rather than as individuals engaged in maximizing their self-interests in the market? The results of our intergenerational distribution case study support the notion that individuals each have a personal social welfare function based on their concept of what they consider to be a fair distribution, reflecting their individual perspective of social justice. This potential for eliciting individual social welfare preferences suggests the need for further research about the community's application of social justice principles to environmental policies with distributional consequences.

The third central question is determining the socio-demographic characteristics upon which distributional preferences are based. This is likely to vary depending on the context of the environmental policy. For example, Loomis (2011) illustrates the application of hedonic analysis to evaluate the effect on house prices of forest fire management decisions in the US, with an emphasis on the distributional impacts of the policy with respect to both income and race. Distributional weights are sensitive to socio-demographic characteristics and there is no doubt that incorporating a range of distributional issues would add to the complexity of a CBA. Nevertheless, exploring the sensitivity of cost–benefit findings to a range of distributional issues will enhance the information available to decision-makers.

The political economy literature (see, for example, Persson and Tabellini 2000; Tabellini 1991) focuses mostly on the allocation process as competition for public resources between cohorts, with an emphasis on the power of voters and lobbying groups. The choice modelling approach to the estimation of social welfare preferences and the incorporation of distributional weights in CBA provides an alternative, and theoretically rigorous, means of incorporating equity considerations in allocation decisions. It also has the advantage of maintaining the distinction between the efficiency and equity aspects of a CBA assessment of policy alternatives.

6.1.1 Intergenerational Distribution Preferences

The distributional preferences reported in Chapter 5 provide a valuable example of distributional preferences which could be incorporated in a CBA. The results suggest positive preferences by the respondent sample towards younger generations. The term 'benevolence' rather than altruism is used to describe these preferences, because altruism, as discussed in Chapter 2, implies an interdependent utility function as opposed to the maximization of a social welfare function. The policy implications of incorporating intergenerational equity preferences in CBAs which assess environmental and natural resource management policies are particularly relevant in terms of the sustainability debate. A central aspect of that debate is the nature of consumption and capital accumulation over time. The magnitude of the positive weighting towards the utility of future generations reported in the results of this choice modelling application gives credence to the notion that individuals derive a positive externality from the welfare of future generations (Arrow et al. 2004).

The question of intergenerational equity can also be approached by comparing the market rate of return on investment (i) and the social rate of interest on consumption (r). If i is greater than r, markets are biased towards insufficient saving and excessive current consumption. Based on the estimation of an intertemporal social welfare function, the social rate of interest on consumption r, is given by the relation: $r = \delta + \eta g$, where δ is the social rate of pure time preference, η is the elasticity of the marginal (social) utility of consumption and g is the rate of growth in aggregate consumption. The relative importance of different generations is affected by the choice of the normative parameters δ and η. The elasticity of the marginal utility of consumption term, η, is interpreted by Arrow et al. (2004) as 'a social preference for equality of consumption among generations'. A low value of η implies that decisions take little heed of whether the future is richer or poorer than the present. Under optimal growth theory, if time discounting is low and society cares little about income inequality, then it will save a great deal for the future and the real return will be low (Nordhaus 2007b).

Arrow et al. (2004) speculate that the value of η is linked to the intertemporal elasticity of consumption. Based on Hall's (1988) time series estimates of the intertemporal elasticity of consumption, they suggest that 'plausible values for η might lie in the range of 2–4'. They suggest that caring about future generations might call for low values of δ, in the range of 0–0.5 per cent per annum. When combined with an assumption of 1.5 per cent per capita growth rate in consumption (g), they arrive at a tentative value for r in the range of 3.0–6.5 per cent per annum.

One example of the importance of this analysis, and the treatment of the gains and losses to future generations, is illustrated in research assessing the implications of global warming and the policy responses to climate change. In analysing the efficient and inefficient approaches to slowing global warming, Nordhaus (2007a) employs an intertemporal social welfare function in the DICE (Dynamic Integrated model of Climate and the Economy) model which compares policy alternatives. In the DICE model, a time discount rate (δ) of 1.5 per cent per year and an elasticity of the marginal utility of consumption (η) of 2.0 are assumed. Nordhaus indicates that these estimates have been revised in the current version of the model and move the model closer to one that displays intergenerational neutrality.[2] He makes the important observation that the two parameters need to be viewed in tandem.[3] For consistency, assuming a value for g of 1.5 per cent per annum (based on Arrow et al. 2004), these estimates would give a value for r of 4.5 per cent per annum.

The disparity in the treatment of future generations in the models assessing the impact of climate change is apparent when the assumptions of the DICE model are compared with those of the Stern Review in the UK (Stern 2007). In his analysis of climate change policy, Stern assumes a discount rate (δ) of 0.1 per cent per year and consumption elasticity (η) of 1.0. Again assuming a value for g of 1.5 per cent per annum, this would yield an estimated value for r of 1.6 per cent per annum and indicates a quite different policy stance toward future generations.[4]

The research by Nordhaus and Stern emphasizes the integral nature of the relationship between the assumptions of the social discount rate and the elasticity of the marginal utility of consumption. Furthermore, it highlights the divergence of assumptions made about the treatment of the utility of future generations in economic modelling. Central to this debate is the ethical judgement about intergenerational equity. As discussed in Chapter 5, low discount rates are not necessarily advantageous to future generations, as they can result in low levels of saving and excessive current consumption.

The approach adopted by this book in estimating distributional preferences suitable for application in a CBA setting provides further insight into the intergenerational preferences of the community. Although the results of the study suggest benevolence towards younger generations, they also highlight the inclusion of intergenerational equity preferences via distributional weights rather than through adjustment to the social discount rate.

The results of both the multinomial logit and the mixed logit models suggest that income may be a significant variable in determining intergenerational distribution preferences. Furthermore, the significant and positive nature of the interaction term between income and the newborn generation and the significant and negative interaction term between income and the aged 50 group, suggest that income is a factor influencing the positive preferences towards the youngest generation evidenced in the intergenerational distribution choice model. These findings about the role of income suggest that respondents may see positive intergenerational preferences towards the youngest generation in a similar manner to positive environmental change. This would support the findings of previous studies indicating that people with higher incomes are willing to pay more for a positive environmental change (see, for example, Fankhauser et al. 1997).

The significance of income in determining preferences with respect to intergenerational distribution also supports the theoretical models in the field of political economy. For example, Tabellini (1991) argues that income levels are significant in a political–economic equilibrium model with overlapping generations. In this model the focus is on the levels of government debt transferred between generations rather than on environmental policy.

Finally, the findings about the disparity between the treatment of gains and losses in determining intergenerational equity preferences are particularly relevant in the context of environmental policy, where policy options may result in losses in utility to future generations. It is possible that these distributional preferences, suggesting an aversion to the costs of environmental degradation being borne by younger generations, may be confounded by bequest, existence and option values which, as discussed in Chapter 1, have been identified in previous studies. Furthermore, some authors argue that environmental damages to future generations cannot be compensated by providing them with some other good (Sen 1982; Barry 1991; Spash 1994; Azar 1999). Further research is required to explore the distinctions between these values and social justice preferences. It may be the case that individuals find difficulty in compartmentalizing the factors that influence their social justice preferences.

The analysis of the heuristics employed by respondents in the intergenerational distribution choice model suggests that a richer understanding of how social justice choices are determined may be gained by applying the method of choice modelling to questions of distribution. However, as with the analysis of the factors influencing social justice preference, more research is needed into the decision-making strategies of respondents. Randall (2002) suggests that the policy process should be thought of as inherently discursive in an open discussion among citizens searching for heuristics we can agree upon and to 'accept that these rules for action are likely to incorporate insights from various moral theories'. The strength of the choice modelling approach to this issue lies with the repeated reminders to respondents of the need to weigh up the competing claims of those who gain and those who lose.

To summarize, responses to the intergenerational distribution choice model indicate distributional weights by the respondent sample which are not equal to one and which reflect benevolent social justice preferences towards the younger generations. The implication of these results is that, in analysing the benefits and costs of environmental policies, those that favour intergenerational transfers of utility towards younger generations may be more likely to be accepted as preferred options by the community.

6.2 OPPORTUNITIES ARISING FROM USING CHOICE MODELLING TO ESTIMATE DISTRIBUTIONAL PREFERENCES

Freeman (1998) defines a social choice as a decision made by society to move to a certain social state. Even doing nothing is a social choice as the alternative of doing something has been rejected. Social choice cannot be avoided. The use of choice modelling to address the distributional consequences of policy alternatives provides another means of eliciting the information required for informed social choice and enhances the potential of CBA as a decision-making tool for policy-makers.

Two alternative forms of social choice procedure are voting on alternative social states or the delegation of authority to make social choices to a politically responsible agency, body or individual. In either case, it is valuable to know if choices actually reflect the underlying preferences or welfare functions of individuals. Yet, neither form of social choice procedure, voting or representation, can in principle determine social orderings and make social choices that conform to the preferences of individuals (Freeman 1998). Musgrave and Musgrave (1989) argue that the state as a cooperative venture among individuals must reflect their interests and concerns. Individuals do not live in isolation but are members of groups and thereby have common concerns. The application of a choice modelling approach to the question of social choice provides an alternative social choice mechanism. It provides the opportunity for the social welfare orderings of the community at large to be voiced. An advantage of this approach is that it takes the value judgement away from policy-makers and economists and places it with the community.

Furthermore, in some environmental policy contexts, the beneficiaries of various programmes and those with vested interests are more likely to be politically organized. They can thus influence political outcomes, whereas the interests of the unorganized general public are neglected (Persson and Tabellini 2000). Choice modelling can have a positive role in overcoming this potential policy bias. Choice modelling is also an appropriate preference elicitation method, as it characterizes the decision-making environment and is able to align itself closely with realistic policy options (Bockstael and McConnell 1999).

A further strength of the application of choice modelling to the estimation of distributional preferences is the ability to analyse the application of social justice principles by the community in determining distributional preferences. For example, the analysis by Scarborough et al. (2009) of heuristics employed by respondents indicates that, in the case of distribution between generations, the classical utilitarian social welfare function may not accurately reflect the social justice principles of the community. This work clearly illustrates the potential of stated choice methods to enhance understanding of distributional preferences and the decision-making strategies employed by respondents in a social welfare context. By further developing the application of choice modelling to distributional concerns, it may be possible to extend the historically rich literature in social welfare. In this context, exploration of divergences between individual decision-making and group decision-making may also yield interesting results. Of particular interest are the heuristics applied by respondents when confronted with potential welfare-changing policies. For example, it may be that respondents display satisficing rather than maximizing behavioural patterns.[5] Linking elicited equity preferences and heuristics to the social welfare literature will enhance our understanding of welfare economics.

While the focus of this book has been environmental policy, the question of the application of distributional weights in CBA is also relevant for many other policy areas. For example, Brent (2003) advocates the application of distributional weights in CBA when assessing health policy alternatives. Consequently, the estimation of distributional weights within other contexts using choice modelling is a potentially fruitful area of future research.

Within the environmental policy framework there are several other important areas where further investigation of perceptions about fair allocations would be informative for policy-makers. For example, the sharing of the cost burden of environmental change between producers, consumers, those with property rights and those responsible for environmental degradation is an important issue. The distribution of benefits and costs between geographic groups is also another equity issue within an environmental context where there is a paucity of knowledge about equity preferences. In practice, policy-makers are required to consider the impact of policy on a myriad of beneficiaries and non-beneficiaries.

There is also a knowledge gap when the social welfare preferences of policy-makers are compared with those of the general community. Hanley and Shogren (2005) acknowledge a problem associated with non-market valuation – namely, that surveying poorly informed people can cause both policy-makers and lobbyists to doubt the value of consumer sovereignty. In a study estimating monetary values for two marine parks, Rogers (2011) found evidence of both convergence and divergence between public and expert values in different instances. Knowledge of the disparity in welfare preferences between policy-makers and the community is a critical element in policy development, consultation and acceptance. It would not solve the problem of whose preferences should be applied, but it would enhance the availability of information for decision-making.

Finally, the focus of this book is on distributive justice, which concerns the final allocation of economic rewards and responsibilities, as opposed to procedural justice, which concerns fair processes. Yet, procedural justice is also important in community assessment of distributional preferences. For example, Syme et al. (1999) found procedural justice was an important aspect of equity considerations for respondents in a study of the allocation of water. A choice modelling approach also has the potential to investigate procedural justice preferences and community perceptions regarding the appropriate processes used to achieve a particular distribution.

The application of the stated preference method of choice modelling to the estimation of distributional preferences is in its infancy. Given this, there is significant potential and opportunity for development of both the methodology and a database aimed at increasing our understanding of community social welfare preferences. These potential advancements also present a number of conceptual and methodological challenges which need to be overcome.

6.3 CHALLENGES IN ESTIMATING DISTRIBUTIONAL PREFERENCES

It is in the nature of research that boundaries must be drawn and that each decision made in constructing a research experiment leads to limitations of the research findings. As with all research, and in particular with attempts to build bridges between complex theoretical questions and the reality of policy environments in which decisions are made, there are a number of significant challenges inherent in the application of the stated preference technique of choice modelling to the estimation of distributional preferences.

6.3.1 The Distinction Between Welfare Maximization and Utility Maximization

Foremost of these challenges influencing the validity of a choice experiment designed to estimate distributional preferences is the assumption that respondents are able to express their preferences from the perspective of social welfare maximization rather than individual utility maximization. The estimation of distributional preferences is dependent on the assumption that respondents are able to adopt a social welfare maximization perspective rather than a utility maximization decision-making framework. An integral part of this problem is the distinction between welfare maximization and interdependent utility functions. For example, if respondents indicate positive preferences towards the utility of another group – for example, a future generation – it is difficult for the researcher to distinguish whether this reflects a respondent who is maximizing personal utility (where the future generation's utility is an interdependent variable), and a respondent who is maximizing social welfare. It is unlikely that respondents are aware of this technical distinction.

A further complication with the assumption of welfare maximization is the consistent theme in the social welfare literature of the application of a 'veil of ignorance' (Rawls 1971). As discussed in Chapter 2, it suggests that individuals, from behind a veil of ignorance that screens knowledge of their future positions, unanimously agree on a redistribution formula (Johansson 1993). This decision about whether to include or omit a veil-of-ignorance assumption presents additional challenges and practical difficulties in eliciting social justice preferences. Depending upon the frame of the experiment, it is unlikely that this assumption will be able to be made by respondents in a choice modelling setting. Hence, distributional preferences are likely to be sensitive to the extent to which self-interest is removed in the framing of an experiment. While the qualitative data in the intergenerational distribution choice experiment suggest that, in general, respondents were able to express their social welfare preferences, the assumption of welfare maximization is challenging. It is difficult to verify to what extent respondents' decision-making is actually conducted in terms of welfare maximization.

It is also likely that there is a difference between how the theory depicts welfare and utility and what the community understands of this distinction. This questions the construct validity of the research. Shadish et al. (2002) suggest that construct validity involves making inferences from the sampling particulars of a study to the higher-order constructs they represent. For the majority of the community, the distinction between welfare as a social ordering and utility maximization as an individual objective is most likely not a concept with which they would be familiar. One possible approach is the adoption of strategies similar to 'cheap talk' strategies which have been applied with some success in addressing hypothetical bias (Cummings and Taylor 1999). This strategy could be employed to remind respondents of the social welfare approach of the preferences being elicited.

Another contentious issue in terms of developing the method of choice modelling in a social welfare context is the problem of determining the reference point for the social welfare function. Within a social welfare context the status quo is a personal subjective opinion regarding the well-being of others. Although it is assumed that respondents have a level of information about the status quo level of utility of the various groups, this level of knowledge is only a perception. However, it is this perception that will form the basis of their preferred distribution and social choice. Further research is required to explore how this reference point varies between respondents and how this affects the estimation of social welfare preferences.

Perhaps one of the most significant challenge facing choice modellers seeking to elicit distributional preferences is determining how to describe changes in utility to respondents. The intergenerational distribution choice experiment used 'smiley faces' in the choice sets to represent changes in utility, and the utility changes were described in term of dollars. The reference key of the questionnaire outlined for respondents the relationship between the smiley faces and the dollars, and respondents were advised that the dollar values represented changes in general well-being in the survey preamble. Retaining money as the numéraire was a pragmatic but limiting decision.

Ideally, an 'index of well-being' may be a more appropriate means of describing utility changes. This has been used in making a theoretical case in an example by Broome (1995) and in empirical research by Cummins (2006). While an index of well-being encourages respondents to think that welfare is broader than dollars and therefore more in line with the notion of welfare in the literature (Sen 1982, 2000), the difficulty and subjectivity in determining an appropriate index, the values of components in the index and descriptors of the index are challenging aspects of the design in a choice experiment. These difficulties are compounded by the need to be aware of the cognitive difficulty for respondents in making complex decisions in an unfamiliar metric.

One well-acknowledged criticism of stated preference methods, including choice modelling, is the distinction between stated preferences and revealed preferences which are supported by actual behaviour. Wills (2006) highlights some of the problems inherent in questioning people about their possible behaviour in hypothetical situations. At the forefront is the problem of communication. There is a risk that respondents will respond to the same description differently for a variety of reasons. This risk is particularly relevant in the case of research designed to elicit distributional preferences.

The choice modelling method places considerable cognitive demands on respondents. Yet, the community does hold social welfare preferences. A critical challenge in developing choice modelling applications to elicit these preferences is that of conveying utility changes to respondents.

6.3.2 Determining Attributes and Levels to Describe Utility Changes

In designing a choice model aimed at eliciting distributional preferences, decisions about the number of attributes and the description of each attribute also involve critical research decisions. Design choices have multiple consequences for the validity of experiments and, as Shadish et al. (2002) highlight, these are not always anticipated.

The social welfare estimates obtained are sensitive to the study design. This limitation is an acknowledged limitation of the methodology (Hanley et al. 2001). The choice of attributes and the levels chosen to represent them and the way in which choices are presented to respondents are not neutral and are likely to affect the marginal welfare values estimated. The issue of framing is another acknowledged limitation of choice modelling as a research method. In this context, in the intergenerational equity case study, the frame of hypothetical policies in an environmental context is likely to have influenced the estimated preferences. For example, it could also be argued that the positive distributional weights towards the younger generations may also reflect a response to uncertainty about the potential utility of future generations.

As indicated in Chapter 4, a number of compromises were made in determining the attributes and their levels for the intergenerational distribution choice model. The decision to limit the generations described by the attributes to those who are currently living had the advantage of enabling the description of the levels to be in terms of current dollars and avoided complications associated with discounting values, which may have challenged the cognitive abilities of respondents. However, limiting the study to distributional preferences between generations with which the respondent may have a closer connection – that is, the generations of children and grandchildren – may have influenced the finding of benevolence towards younger generations. It would be interesting to extend the time horizon of the research and examine the sensitivity of the findings to generations further removed from respondents.

It is also unknown how the descriptors given for each age group may have influenced the choices of respondents. For example, the use of 'newborns' to describe the youngest of the generations described by the attributes in the choice sets may have distorted the preferences elicited by respondents. Respondents may possess positive feelings toward babies which may have confounded the results. Hence the findings are sensitive to the choice of attributes and their levels.

Finally, the interpretation of distributional preferences should be treated cautiously, as it is possible that environmental preferences may have been enmeshed in the distributional preferences. For example, in the intergenerational distribution choice experiment, it is possible that environmental preferences are also embedded in the intergenerational distribution preferences and that there is some double counting within these results. As indicated in Chapter 4, previous research has indicated that current generations have positive bequest and options values toward the environment. These values may also be incorporated in their preferences towards future generations. The findings with respect to intergenerational distribution may be different in alternative contexts.

6.3.3 Incorporating Efficiency Cost

As discussed, one of the key debates in the literature about distributional weighting is the possible trade-off confronting policy-makers between efficiency and equity objectives. Redistribution and the incorporation of equity in policy analysis are likely to involve an efficiency cost. The incorporation of an efficient cost in a choice model designed to estimate distributional preferences is a challenge, but has the potential to provide a fruitful area of research which would enhance our understanding of community preferences about this balancing of policy objectives. Designing a choice experiment which not only attempts to elicit the 'sharing of the pie' but also the total 'size of the pie' is challenging.

6.3.4 Sensitivity to Choice of Numéraire in Estimating Marginal Utility

As outlined in Chapter 2, distributional weights are highly dependent on the marginal utility of consumption of various groups within society. The marginal utility is also likely to be sensitive to the choice of numéraire. For example, in an environmental context, the marginal utility of income may differ from the marginal utility of an environmental good. Exploration of this sensitivity will also enhance understanding of distributional preferences.

The possible decomposition of the two components of the distributional weights also presents a further challenge and research opportunity. As the theory outlined in Chapter 2 highlights, the social justice preferences of respondents are influenced by how they rank a particular group or individual in their social welfare function, and how they assess the value of a marginal change in consumption for the particular group or individual. As the two components of the distributional weight are both incorporated in the social marginal rate of substitution, extracting to what extent estimated weights are influenced by assumptions regarding variance in the marginal utility for different groups and to what extent they reflect pure welfare preferences presents a challenge for the researcher. Also influencing this decomposition is the issue that both welfare rankings and marginal utilities are likely to vary depending on the numéraire.

In summary, there are a number of significant challenges associated with the application of choice modelling to the estimation of distributional preferences. In particular, the challenges are the consequence of the desire to build bridges between complex theoretical constructs and practical policy outcomes. However, while mindful of these challenges, the potential for enhancing the capacity of CBA as a decision-making tool which encompasses both equity and efficiency in policy analysis is significant.

6.4 FINAL CONCLUSIONS

In the development of economic policy, questions inevitably arise about the distribution of resources. Given that the aim of CBA is to provide a ranking of policy proposals, the analysis of policy options requires two strands, addressing both the efficiency and the equity implications of policy alternatives. Nobel prize-winning economist Amaryta Sen argues that a central aspect of the analysis of policy alternatives is identifying whether a particular social change will enhance justice (Sen 2009). Yet, historically, it is with some reluctance that economists have addressed equity issues in policy analysis. This book seeks to put the issue of incorporating distributional changes in the decision-making calculus firmly on the research agenda. There is an argument that the question of incorporating equity in policy analysis is beyond the scope of economics – economists are normally considered more comfortable in dealing with efficiency. However, increasingly, for economic analysis of environmental change to be comprehensive and relevant for both policy-makers and the community, it is imperative that both equity and efficiency are incorporated in policy analysis. Although the difficulties of incorporating equity consideration in CBA are acknowledged, the importance of improving knowledge of social justice preferences is stressed. This issue is particularly crucial in the assessment of the impact of environmental and natural resource management policy.

This book addresses the equity issue by showing that it is possible to use the stated preference technique of choice modelling to derive distributional weights applicable for CBA. Stated preference methods, such as choice modelling, have the potential to contribute to our understanding of the distributional preferences held by the community. An advantage of this approach is that it takes the value judgement away from the policy-maker and the economist and places it with the community. However, more research is needed to further develop these methods in a social welfare context.

The sensitivity of policy interventions is important because the political acceptability and effectiveness of any policy will depend on the distribution of the costs and benefits. Economists face considerable challenges in providing policy-makers with decision-making strategies that incorporate both efficiency and equity. The application of distributional weights in CBA provides a conceptually rigorous decision-making framework which meets these criteria.

The case study outlined demonstrates that it is possible to estimate distributional weights suitable for application in a CBA setting and that the community holds identifiable social welfare preferences. Resource use involves choices about 'for whom' as well as 'what'. Given that economics is about choice, then the profession is obliged to consider both equity and efficiency. People do hold preferences over both utility and welfare, and the application of choice modelling to the estimation of social welfare preferences is one way of overcoming economists' traditional concerns about the subjectivity associated with welfare estimates by exploring people's preferences in that space.

The incorporation of equity in CBA and policy analysis is a complex issue. However, it is an area where economists should continue to strive to develop and refine decision-making tools. While stated preference methods such as choice modelling have exciting potential in terms of improving our understanding of distributional preferences, these developments also raise significant issues where further research and debate are required.

NOTES

1. The terms 'citizen' and 'consumer' have also been used in the literature (Blamey et al. 1995; Rolfe and Bennett 1996; Blamey et al. 1996). This discussion is centred on contingent valuation studies based on the assumption that respondents are maximizing utility functions. A clear distinction needs to be drawn between utility maximization and welfare maximization, hence the adoption of Nyborg's terminology.
2. Nordhaus also takes care to emphasize that these estimates measure the importance of the welfare of future generations relative to the present, and refers to future utility, not future goods or dollars, as this study has also emphasized.
3. In the DICE model the same outcome is achieved with the assumption of a lower discount rate of 0.1 per cent and a higher marginal utility of consumption of 2.9.
4. Responses to these assumptions in the Stern Review are divided and are summarized concisely by Baker et al. (2008).

5. Satisficing is an alternative conception of rational behaviour to optimizing. It refers to the possibility that respondents may choose an option that meets or exceeds specified criteria but is not necessarily either unique or the best (Simon 1956).

Bibliography

Adamowicz, W., P. Boxall, M. Williams and J. Louviere (1998), 'Stated preference approaches for measuring passive use values: choice experiments and contingent valuation', *American Journal of Agricultural Economics*, **80** (1), 64–76.

Adamowicz, W., P. Boxall, J. Louviere, J. Swait and M. Williams (1999), 'Stated-Preference Methods for Valuing Environmental Amenities', in I. Bateman and K. Willis (eds), *Valuing Environmental Preferences*, Oxford: Oxford University Press, pp. 460–79.

Adamowicz, W., J. Louviere and M. Williams (1994), 'Combining revealed and stated preference methods for valuing environmental amenities', *Journal of Environmental Economics and Management*, **26**, 271–92.

Adelman, I. and C. Morris (1973), *Economic Growth and Economic Equity in Developing Countries*, Stanford: Stanford University Press.

Adler, M. and E. Posner (1999), 'Rethinking cost–benefit analysis', *The Yale Law Journal*, **109** (2), 164–247.

Agyeman, J., R. Bullard and B. Evans (eds) (2003), *Just Sustainabilities: Development in an Unequal World*, London: Earthscan.

Ahluwalia, M. (1975), 'Income Inequality: Some Dimensions of the Problem', in H. Chenery (ed.), *Redistribution with Growth*, Oxford: Oxford University Press, pp. 3–37.

Alfnes, F., A. Guttormsen, G. Steine and K. Kolstad (2006), 'Consumers' willingness to pay for the color of salmon: a choice experiment with real economic incentives', *American Journal of Agricultural Economics*, **88** (4), 1050–61.

Arrow, K. (1963), *Social Choice and Individual Values*, New York: Wiley.

Arrow, K. (1984), *Social Choice and Justice*, Oxford: Basil Blackwell.

Arrow, K. and M. Kurz (1970), *Public Investment, The Rate of Return, and Optimal Fiscal Policy*, Washington, DC: Resources for the Future.

Arrow, K., W. Cline, K.-G. Mäler, M. Munaginghe and J. Stiglitz (1996), 'Intertemporal Equity, Discounting, and Economic Efficiency', in J. Bruce, H. Lee and E. Haites (eds), *Climate Change 1995*, Cambridge: Cambridge University Press, pp. 130–44.

Arrow, K., P. Dasgupta, L. Goulder, G. Daily, P. Ehrlich, G. Heal, S. Levin, K.-G. Mäler, S. Schneider, D. Starrett and B. Walker (2004), 'Are we consuming too much?', *Journal of Economic Perspectives*, **18** (3), 147–72.

Atkinson, G., F. Machado and S. Mourato (2000), 'Balancing competing principles of environmental equity', *Environment and Planning*, **32**, 1791–806.

Attfield, R. (1983), *The Ethics of Environmental Concern*, Oxford: Basil Blackwell.

Australian Bureau of Statistics (ABS) (2001), *Census of Population and Housing*, Canberra: Commonwealth of Australia.

Azar, C. (1999), 'Weight factors in cost–benefit analysis of climate change', *Environmental and Resource Economics*, **13** (3), 249–68.

Baker, R., A. Barker, A. Johnston and M. Kohlhaas (2008), *The Stern Review: An Assessment of its Methodology*, Melbourne: Productivity Commission Staff Working Paper.

Banuri, K., K.-G. Mäler, M. Grubb, H. Jacobson and F. Yamin (1996), 'Equity and Social Considerations', in J. Bruce, H. Lee and E. Haites (eds), *Climate Change 1995*, Cambridge: Cambridge University Press, pp. 79–124.

Barry, B. (1989), *Theories of Justice*, London: Harvester Wheatsheaf.

Barry, B. (1991), *Liberty and Justice: Essays in Political Theory*, Oxford: Clarendon Press.

Basu, K. (1980), *Revealed Preference of Government*, Cambridge: Cambridge University Press.

Bateman, I., R. Carson, B. Day, W. Hanemann, N. Hanley, T. Hett, L. Jones, G. Loomes, S. Mourato, E. Ozdemiroglu, D. Pearce, R. Sugden and J. Swanson (2002), *Economic Valuation with Stated Preference Techniques*, Cheltenham, UK and Northampton, MA, USA: Edward Elgar.

Belshaw, C. (2001), *Environmental Philosophy: Reason, Nature and Human Concern*, Chesham, UK: Acumen.

Bennett, J. (2003), 'Economics and the Environment', in I. McAllister, S. Dowrick and R. Hassan (eds), *The Cambridge Handbook of Social Sciences in Australia*, Cambridge: Cambridge University Press, pp. 45–59.

Bennett, J. (2005), 'Australasian environmental economics: contributions, conflicts, and "cop-outs"', *The Australian Journal of Agricultural and Resource Economics*, **49** (3), 243–61.

Bennett, J. and W. Adamowicz (2001), 'Some Fundamentals of Environmental Choice Modelling', in J. Bennett and R. Blamey (eds), *The Choice Modelling Approach to Environmental Valuation*, Cheltenham, UK and Northampton, MA, USA: Edward Elgar, pp. 37–69.

Bennett, J. and R. Blamey (eds) (2001), *The Choice Modelling Approach to Environmental Valuation*, Cheltenham, UK and Northampton, MA, USA: Edward Elgar.

Bennett, J., J. Rolfe and M. Morrison (2001), 'Remnant Vegetation and Wetlands Protection: Non-market Valuation', in J. Bennett and R. Blamey (eds), *The Choice Modelling Approach to Environmental Valuation*, Cheltenham, UK and Northampton, MA, USA: Edward Elgar, pp. 93–114.

Bentham, J. (1789), *An Introduction to the Principles of Morals and Legislation*, reprinted in J. Burns and H. Hart (eds) (1970), London: Athlone.

Bergson, A. (1938), 'A reformulation of certain aspects of welfare economics', *Quarterly Journal of Economics*, **52** (2), 310–34.

Bhat, C. (1997), 'An endogenous segmentation mode choice model with an application to intercity travel', *Transportation Science*, **31** (1), 34–48.

Bhat, C. (2001), 'Quasi-random maximum simulated likelihood estimation of the mixed multinomial logit model', *Transportation Research*, **35** (7), 677–95.

Blackorby, C. and D. Donaldson (1987), 'Welfare ratios and distributionally sensitive cost–benefit analysis', *Journal of Public Economics*, **34**, 265–90.

Blackorby, C. and D. Donaldson (1990), 'The case against the use of the sum of compensating variations in cost–benefit analysis', *Canadian Journal of Economics*, **13**, 471–79.

Blamey, R., M. Common and J. Quiggin (1995), 'Respondents to contingent valuation surveys: consumers or citizens?', *Australian Journal of Agricultural Economics*, **39** (3), 263–88.

Blamey, R., M. Common and J. Quiggin (1996), 'Respondents to contingent valuation surveys: consumers or citizens? – Reply', *Australian Journal of Agricultural Economics*, **40** (2), 135–38.

Blamey, R., J. Gordon and R. Chapman (1999), 'Choice modelling: assessing the environmental values of water supply options', *The Australian Journal of Agricultural and Resource Economics*, **43** (3), 337–57.

Blamey, R., J. Louviere and J. Bennett (2001), 'Choice Set Design', in J. Bennett and R. Blamey (eds), *The Choice Modelling Approach to Environmental Valuation*, Cheltenham, UK and Northampton, MA, USA: Edward Elgar, pp. 133–56.

Boadway, R. (1974), 'The welfare foundations of cost–benefit analysis', *Economic Journal*, **84**, 926–39.

Boadway, R. and N. Bruce (1984), *Welfare Economics*, Oxford: Basil Blackwell.

Bockstael, N. and K. McConnell (1999), 'The Behavioural Basis of Non-Market Valuation', in J. Herriges and C. Kling (eds), *Valuing Recreation and the Environment, Revealed Preference Methods in Theory and Practice*, Cheltenham, UK and Northampton, MA, USA: Edward Elgar, pp. 1–32.

Bojer, H. (2003), *Distributional Justice: Theory and Measurement*, London: Routledge.

Boxall, P., W. Adamowicz, J. Swait, M. Williams and J. Louviere (1996), 'A comparison of stated preference methods for environmental valuation', *Ecological Economics*, **18**, 243–53.

Brent, R. (1991), 'On the estimation technique to reveal government distributional weights', *Applied Economics*, **23**, 985–92.

Brent, R. (2003), *Cost–Benefit Analysis and Health Care Evaluations*, Cheltenham, UK and Northampton, MA, USA: Edward Elgar.

Brent, R.J. (2006), *Applied Cost–Benefit Analysis*, 2nd edition, Cheltenham, UK and Northampton, MA, USA: Edward Elgar.

Broome, J. (1995), *Weighing Goods*, Oxford: Basil Blackwell.

Brown, G. and J. Shogren (2005), 'Economics of the Endangered Species Act', in R. Stavins (ed.), *Economics of the Environment: Selected Readings*, 5th edition, New York: W.W. Norton, pp. 514–32.

Burton, M., D. Rigby, T. Young and S. James (2001), 'Consumer attitudes to genetically modified organisms in food in the UK', *European Review of Agricultural Economics*, **28** (4), 479–98.

Campbell, H. and R. Brown (2003), *Benefit–Cost Analysis*, Cambridge: Cambridge University Press.

Chichilnisky, G. (1996), 'An axiomatic approach to sustainable development', *Social Choice and Welfare*, **13**, 219–48.

Collard, D. (1978), *Altruism and Economy*, Oxford: Martin Robertson.

Commonwealth of Australia (2007), *Intergenerational Report*, Canberra: Commonwealth of Australia.

Commonwealth of Australia (2010), *Intergenerational Report*, Canberra: Commonwealth of Australia.

Cowell, F. and K. Gardiner (1999), *Welfare Weights*, Report to the UK Office of Fair Trading, United Kingdom.

Cummings, R. and L. Taylor (1999), 'Unbiased value estimates for environmental goods: a cheap talk design for the contingent valuation method', *American Economic Review*, **89** (3), 649–65.

Cummins, R. (2006), *Australian Unity Wellbeing Index*, Report 14.1, Deakin University, http://acqol.deakin.edu.au/instruments/wellbeing_index.htm, accessed 14 January 2008.

Dasgupta, P., A. Sen and S. Marglin (1972), *Guidelines for Project Evaluation*, New York: United Nations.

Department of Finance and Administration (2006), *Introduction to Cost–Benefit Analysis and Alternative Evaluation Methodologies*, Canberra: Australian Government.

Dey, A. and R. Mukerjee (1999), *Fractional Factorial Plans*, New York: John Wiley & Sons.

Dorfman, R. (1977), 'Incidence of the benefits and costs of environmental programs', *American Economic Review*, **67** (1), 333–40.

Drèze, J. (1998), 'Distribution matters in cost–benefit analysis: comment on K.A. Brekke', *Journal of Public Economics*, **70**, 485–8.

Drèze, J. and N. Stern (1987), 'The Theory of Cost–Benefit Analysis', in A. Auerbach and M. Feldstein (eds), *Handbook of Public Economics, Vol. 11*, Amsterdam: Elsevier Science, pp. 909–89.

Drèze, J. and N. Stern (1994), 'Shadow prices and markets: policy reform, shadow prices and market prices', in R. Layard and S. Glaister (eds), *Cost–Benefit Analysis*, Cambridge: Cambridge University Press, pp. 59–99.

Edgeworth, F.Y. (1881), *Mathematical Psychics*, London: Kegan Paul.

Ekins, P. (2000), *Economic Growth and Environmental Sustainability: The Prospects for Green Growth*, London: Routledge.

Elster, J. (1992), *Local Justice: How Institutions Allocate Scarce Goods and Necessary Burdens*, Cambridge: Cambridge University Press.

Fankhauser, S., R. Tol and D. Pearce (1997), 'The aggregation of climate change damages: a welfare theoretic approach', *Environmental and Resource Economics*, **10** (3), 249–66.

Farrow, S. and M. Toman (1998), 'Using Environmental Benefit–Cost Analysis to Improve Government Performance', Resources for the Future Discussion Paper, 99-11.

Freeman, A. (1998), *The Economic Approach to Environmental Policy*, Cheltenham, UK and Northampton, MA, USA: Edward Elgar.

Freeman, A. (2003), 'Economic Valuation: What and Why', in P. Champ, K. Boyle and T. Brown (eds), *A Primer on Nonmarket Valuation*, London: Kluwer, pp. 1–25.

Garrod, G. and K. Willis (1999), *Economic Valuation of the Environment*, Cheltenham, UK and Northampton, MA, USA: Edward Elgar.

Garnaut, R. (2008), *The Garnaut Climate Change Review*, Cambridge: Cambridge University Press.

Gollier, C. (2002), 'Time horizon and the discount rate', *Journal of Economic Theory*, **107**, 463–73.

Greene, W., D. Hensher and J. Rose (2005), 'Using Classical Simulation-Based Estimators to Estimate Individual WTP Values', in R. Scarpa and A. Alberini (eds), *Applications of Simulation Methods in Environmental and Resource Economics*, Dordrecht: Springer, pp. 17–33.

Haab, T. and K. McConnell (2002), *Valuing Environmental and Natural Resources*, Cheltenham, UK and Northampton, MA, USA: Edward Elgar.

Hall, R. (1988), 'Intertemporal substitution in consumption', *The Journal of Political Economy*, **96** (2), 339–57.

Hanemann, W. (1984), 'Discrete/continuous models of consumer demand', *Econometrica*, **52** (3), 541–61.

Hanemann, W. (2005), 'Valuing the Environment through Contingent Valuation', in R. Stavins (ed.), *Economics of the Environment: Selected Readings*, 5th edition, New York: W.W. Norton, pp. 146–72.

Hanley, N. and J. Shogren (2005), 'Is cost–benefit analysis anomaly proof?', *Environmental & Resource Economics*, **32**, 13–34.

Hanley, N. and C. Spash (1993), *Cost–Benefit Analysis and the Environment*, Aldershot, UK and Brookfield, US: Edward Elgar.

Hanley, N., S. Mourato and R. Wright (2001), 'Choice modelling approaches: a superior alternative for environmental valuation?', *Journal of Economic Surveys*, **15** (3), 435–62.

Hanley, N., J. Shogren and B. White (2007), *Environmental Economics: In Theory and Practice*, 2nd edition, Hampshire: Palgrave Macmillan.

Harberger, A. (1978), 'On the use of distributional weights in social cost–benefit analysis', *Journal of Political Economy*, **86** (supplement), 87–120.

Harberger, A. (1984), 'Basic needs versus distributional weights in social cost–benefit analysis', *Economic Development and Cultural Change*, **32**, 455–74.

Hausman, J. and D. McFadden (1984), 'Specification tests for the multinomial logit model', *Econometrica*, **52** (5), 1219–40.

Haveman, R. (1965), *Water Resource Investment and the Public Interest*, Nashville, USA: Vanderbilt University Press.

Hediger, W. (2000), 'Sustainable development and social welfare', *Ecological Economics*, **32**, 481–92.

Hensher, D., J. Rose and W. Greene (2005), *Applied Choice Analysis*, Cambridge: Cambridge University Press.

Hicks, J. (1943), 'The four consumers' surpluses', *Review of Economic Studies*, **11**, 31–41.

HM Treasury (2003), *The Green Book: Appraisal and Evaluation in Central Government*, London, http://www.hm-treasury.gov.uk/data_greenbook_index.htm, accessed 12 April 2011.

Howarth, R. and R. Norgaard (1990), 'Intergenerational resource rights, efficiency, and social optimality', *Land Economics*, **66** (1), 181–91.

Howarth, R. and R. Norgaard (1992), 'Environmental valuation under sustainable development', *American Economic Review*, **82** (2), 473–7.

Islam, S., M. Munasinghe and M. Clarke (2003), 'Making long-term economic growth more sustainable: evaluating the costs and benefits', *Ecological Economics*, **47**, 149–66.

Johansson, P.-O. (1987), *The Economic Theory and Measurement of Environmental Benefits*, Cambridge: Cambridge University Press.

Johansson, P.-O. (1991), *An Introduction to Modern Welfare Economics*, Cambridge: Cambridge University Press.

Johansson, P.-O. (1993), *Cost–Benefit Analysis of Environmental Change*, Cambridge: Cambridge University Press.

Johansson, P.-O. (1998), 'Does the choice of numéraire matter in cost–benefit analysis?', *Journal of Public Economics*, **70**, 489–93.

Johansson-Stenman, O. (2005), 'Distributional weights in cost–benefit analysis', *Land Economics*, **81** (3), 337–52.

Johansson-Stenman, O., F. Carlsson and D. Daruvala (2002), 'Measuring future grandparents' preferences for equality and relative standing', *The Economic Journal*, **112**, 362–83.

Johansson-Stenman, Olof and Peter Martinsson (2008), 'Are some lives more valuable? An ethical preferences approach', *Journal of Health Economics*, **27** (3), 739–52.

Kahn, J. (2005), *The Economic Approach to Environmental and Natural Resources*, 3rd edition, London: Thomson.

Kahneman, D. and A. Tversky (1979), 'Prospect theory: an analysis of decision under risk', *Econometrica*, **47** (2), 263–91.

Kahneman, D., I. Ritov and D. Schkade (2000), 'Economic Preferences or Attitude Expressions? An Analysis of Dollar Responses to Public Issues', in D. Kahneman and A. Tversky (eds), *Choices, Values and Frames*, Cambridge: Cambridge University Press, pp. 642–72.

Kaplow, L. (1996), 'The optimal supply of public goods and the distortionary cost of taxation', *National Tax Journal*, **49** (4), 513–33.

Kneese, A. and W. Schulze (1985), 'Ethics and Environmental Economics', in A. Kneese and J. Sweeney (eds), *Handbook of Natural Resource and Energy Economics*, Amsterdam: Elsevier Science, pp. 191–220.

Konow, J. (2001), 'Fair and square: the four sides of distributive justice', *Journal of Economic Behaviour and Organization*, **46**, 137–64.

Krinsky, I. and A. Robb (1986), 'On approximating the statistical properties of elasticities', *The Review of Economics and Statistics*, **68** (4), 715–19.

Kriström, B. (2006), 'Framework for Assessing the Distribution of Financial Effects of Environmental Policy', in Y. Serret and N. Johnstone (eds), *The Distributional Effects of Environmental Policy*, Cheltenham, UK and Northampton, MA, USA: Edward Elgar, pp. 79–136.

Kriström, B. and T. Laitila (2003), 'Stated Preference Methods for Environmental Valuation: A Critical Look', in H. Folmer and T. Tietenberg (eds), *The International Yearbook of Environmental and Resource Economics 2003/2004: A Survey of Current Issues*, Cheltenham, UK and Northampton, MA, USA: Edward Elgar, pp. 305–30.

Krutilla, J. (1967), 'Conservation reconsidered', *American Economic Review*, **54** (4), 777–86.

Krysiak, F. and D. Krysiak (2006), 'Sustainability with uncertain future preferences', *Environmental & Resource Economics*, **33**, 511–31.

Lancaster, K. (1966), 'A new approach to consumer theory', *Journal of Political Economy*, **74**, 132–57.

Lancaster, K. (1971), *Consumer Demand: A New Approach*, New York: Columbia University Press.

Lange, A. (2006), 'The impact of equity-preferences on the stability of international environmental agreements', *Environmental & Resource Economics*, **34**, 247–67.

Lazari, A. and D. Anderson (1994), 'Designs of discrete choice set experiments for establishing both attribute and availability cross effects', *Journal of*

Marketing Research, **XXXI**, 375–83.

Little, I. and J. Mirrlees (1974), *Project Appraisal and Planning for Developing Countries*, London: Heinemann.

Little, I. and J. Mirrlees (1994), 'The Costs and Benefits of Analysis: Project Appraisal and Planning Twenty Years on', in R. Layard and S. Glaister (eds), *Cost–Benefit Analysis*, Cambridge: Cambridge University Press, pp. 199–234.

Long, J. (1997), *Regression Models for Categorical and Limited Dependent Variables*, Thousand Oaks, CA: SAGE Publications.

Loomis, J. (2011), 'Incorporating distributional issues into Benefit–Cost Analysis: why, how, and two empirical examples using non-market valuation', *Journal of Benefit–Cost Analysis*, **2** (1), Article 5.

Louviere, J. (2001), 'Choice Experiments: An Overview of Concepts and Issues', in J. Bennett and R. Blamey (eds), *The Choice Modelling Approach to Environmental Valuation*, Cheltenham, UK and Northampton, MA, USA: Edward Elgar, pp. 13–36.

Louviere, J. (2006), 'What you don't know might hurt you: some unresolved issues in the design and analysis of discrete choice experiments', *Environmental & Resource Economics*, **34**, 173–88.

Louviere, J. and D. Hensher (1982), 'On the design and analysis of simulated choice or allocation experiments in travel choice modelling', *Transportation Research Record*, **890**, 11–17.

Louviere, J. and G. Woodworth (1983), 'Design and analysis of simulated consumer choice or allocation experiments: an approach based on aggregate data', *Journal of Marketing Research*, **20**, 350–67.

Louviere, J., D. Hensher and J. Swait (2000), *Stated Choice Methods*, Cambridge: Cambridge University Press.

Luce, R.D. (1959), *Individual Choice Behaviour: A Theoretical Analysis*, New York: Wiley.

Mackay, H. (1997), *Generations: Baby Boomers, Their Parents & Their Children*, Sydney: Macmillan.

McFadden, D. (1974), 'Conditional Logit Analysis of Qualitative Choice Behaviour', in P. Zarembka (ed.), *Frontiers in Econometrics*, New York: Academic Press, pp. 105–42.

McFadden, D. and K. Train (2000), 'Mixed MNL models for discrete response', *Journal of Applied Econometrics*, **15**, 447–70.

Maler, K.-G. (1985), 'Welfare Economics and the Environment', in A. Kneese and J. Sweeney (eds), *Handbook of Natural Resource and Energy Economics*, Amsterdam: Elsevier Science, pp. 3–60.

Markandya, A. (1998), 'Poverty, income distribution and policy making', *Environmental and Resource Economics*, **11** (3–4), 459–72.

Marshall, A. (1890), *Principles of Economics*, London: Macmillan.

Medin, H., K. Nyborg and I. Bateman (2001), 'The assumption of equal marginal utility of income: how much does it matter?', *Ecological Economics*, **36**, 397–411.

Mill, J. (1863), *Utilitarianism*, London: Parker, Son and Bourn.

Mirrlees, J. (1971), 'An exploration in the theory of optimum income taxation', *Review of Economic Studies*, **38**, 175–208.

Mishan, E. (1981), *Introduction to Normative Economics*, New York: Oxford University Press.

Mishan, E. (1988), *Cost–Benefit Analysis*, London: Unwin Hyman.

Mitchell, R. and R. Carson (1989), *Using Surveys to Value Public Goods: The Contingent Valuation Method*, Washington, DC: Resources for the Future.

Mitchell, R. and R. Carson (1995), 'Current Issues in the Design, Administration, and Analysis of Contingent Valuation Surveys', in P.-O. Johansson, B. Kristöm and K.-G. Mäler (eds), *Current Issues in Environmental Economics*, Manchester: Manchester University Press, pp. 10–34.

Morrison, M. and O. Bergland (2006), 'Prospects for the use of choice modelling for benefit transfer', *Ecological Economics*, **60**, 420–28.

Morrison, M., R. Blamey, J. Bennett and J. Louviere (1996), 'A Comparison of Stated Preference Techniques for Estimating Environmental Values', Research Report No. 1, Canberra: School of Economics and Management, University of New South Wales.

Mueller, D. (1989), *Public Choice II*, Cambridge: Cambridge University Press.

Musgrave, R. and P. Musgrave (1989), *Public Finance in Theory and Practice*, 5th edition, New York: McGraw-Hill.

Myles, G. (1995), *Public Economics*, Cambridge: Cambridge University Press.

Nash, C., D. Pearce and J. Stanley (1975), 'An evaluation of cost–benefit analysis criteria', *Scottish Journal of Political Economy*, **22** (2), 121–34.

Ng, Y.-K. (1983), *Welfare Economics: Introduction and Development of Basic Concepts*, revised edition, London: Macmillan.

Ng, Y.-K. (2000a), 'The optimal size of public spending and the distortionary cost of taxation', *National Tax Journal*, **53** (2), 253–72.

Ng, Y.-K. (2000b), *Efficiency, Equality and Public Policy – With a Case For Higher Public Spending*, New York: MacMillan Press.

Nordhaus, W. (2007a), 'The Challenge of Global Warming: Economic Models and Environmental Policy', http://nordhaus.econ.yale.edu/recent_stuff.html, accessed 14 January 2008.

Nordhaus, W. (2007b), 'Critical assumptions in the Stern review on climate change', *Science*, **317**, 201–2.

Norton, B. (1987), *Why Preserve Natural Variety?*, Princeton, NJ: Princeton University Press.

Nyborg, K. (2000), 'Homo economicus and homo politicus: interpretation and aggregation of environmental values', *Journal of Economic Behaviour and*

Organization, **42**, 305–22.

Pannell, D. and S. Schilizzi (2006), 'Time and Discounting in Economic Decision Making', in D. Pannell and S. Schilizzi (eds), *Economics and the Future: Time and Discounting in Private and Public Decision Making*, Cheltenham, UK and Northampton, MA USA: Edward Elgar, pp. 1–12.

Parfit, D. (1976), 'Rights, Interests and Possible People', in S. Gorovitz (ed.), *Moral Problems in Medicine*, Englewood Cliffs, NJ: Prentice-Hall, pp. 369–75.

Parfit, D. (1982), 'Future generations: further problems', *Philosophy and Public Affairs*, **11** (2), 113–72.

Pearce, D. (1976), *Environmental Economics*, London: Longman.

Pearce, D. (1983), *Cost–Benefit Analysis*, London: Macmillan Press.

Pearce, D. (1993), *Economic Values and the Natural World*, London: Earthscan.

Pearce, D. (2006), 'Framework for Assessing the Distribution of Environmental Quality', in Y. Serret and N. Johnstone (eds), *The Distributional Effects of Environmental Policy*, Cheltenham, UK and Northampton, MA, USA: Edward Elgar, pp. 23–78.

Pearce, D. and E. Barbier (2000), *Blueprint for a Sustainable Economy*, London: Earthscan.

Persson, T. and G. Tabellini (2000), *Political Economics, Explaining Economic Policy*, Cambridge, MA: The MIT Press.

Pezzey, J. (1989), 'Economic Analysis of Sustainable Growth and Sustainable Development', World Bank Environment Department Working Paper 15, Washington, DC: World Bank.

Pezzey, J. and M. Toman (2002), *The Economics of Sustainability*, Burlington: Ashgate.

Pigou, A. (1920), *The Economics of Welfare*, London: Macmillan.

Poe, G., K. Giraud and J. Loomis (2005), 'Computational methods for measuring the difference of empirical distributions', *American Journal of Agricultural Economics*, **87** (2), 353–65.

Popp, D. (2001), 'Altruism and the demand for environmental quality', *Land Economics*, **77** (3), 339–49.

Raktoe, B., A. Hedayat and W. Federer (1981), *Factorial Designs*, New York: John Wiley & Sons.

Ramsey, F. (1928), 'A mathematical theory of savings', *Economic Journal*, **38**, 543–9.

Randall, A. (1987), *Resource Economics: An Economic Approach to Natural Resource and Environmental Policy*, 2nd edition, New York: John Wiley.

Randall, A. (2002), 'Benefit–Cost Considerations should be Decisive when there is Nothing More Important at Stake', in D. Bromley and J. Paavola (eds), *Economics, Ethics and Environmental Policy*, Oxford: Blackwell Publishing, pp. 53–68.

Randall, A. (2006), 'Discounting future prospects, and the quest for sustainability', in D.J. Pannell and G. Schilizzi (eds), *Economics and the Future: Time and Discounting in Private and Public Decision Making*, Cheltenham, UK and Northampton, MA, USA: Edward Elgar, pp. 97–120.

Rawls, J. (1971), *A Theory of Justice*, Cambridge, MA: Harvard University Press.

Rawls, J. (2001), *Justice as Fairness: A Restatement*, edited by Erin Kelly, Cambridge, MA: Harvard University Press.

Rescher, N. (2002), *Fairness*, New Brunswick, NJ: Transaction Publishers.

Revelt, D. and K. Train (1998), 'Incentives for appliance efficiency in a competitive energy environment: random parameters logit models of households' choices', *Review of Economics and Statistics*, **80** (4), 647–57.

Robbins, L. (1932), *An Essay on the Nature and Significance of Economic Science*, London: Macmillan.

Roberts, K. (1980a), 'Possibility theorems with interpersonally comparable welfare levels', *Review of Economic Studies*, **47**, 409–20.

Roberts, K. (1980b), 'Interpersonal comparability and social choice theory', *Review of Economic Studies*, **47**, 421–39.

Rodríguez, E. and J. Pinto (2000), 'The social value of health programmes: is age a relevant factor?', *Health Economics*, **9**, 611–21.

Roe, B., K. Boyle and M. Teisl (1996), 'Using conjoint analysis to derive estimates of compensating variation', *Journal of Environmental Economics and Management*, **31**, 145–59.

Rogers, A. (2011), 'Is Choice Modelling Really Necessary? Public versus Expert Values for Marine Reserves in Western Australia', Paper presented at AARES 55th Annual Conference, Melbourne, Australia.

Rolfe, J. and J. Bennett (1996), 'Respondents to contingent valuation surveys; consumers or citizens – a comment', *Australian Journal of Agricultural Economics*, **40** (2), 129–33.

Rose, A., B. Stevens, J. Edmonds and M. Wise (1998), 'International equity and differentiation in global warming', *Environmental and Resource Economics*, **12**, 25–51.

Rosen, S. (1974), 'Hedonic prices and implicit markets: product differentiation in pure competition', *Journal of Political Economy*, **82** (1), 34–55.

Sagoff, M. (1988), *The Economy of the Earth*, New York: Cambridge University Press.

Samuelson, P. (1947), *Foundations of Economic Analysis*, Cambridge, MA: Harvard University Press.

Samuelson, W. and R. Zeckhauser (1988), 'Status quo bias in decision making', *Journal of Risk and Uncertainty*, **1**, 7–59.

Scarborough, H. (2011), 'Intergenerational equity and the social discount rate', *Australian Journal of Agricultural and Resource Economics*, **55** (2), 164–77.

Scarborough, H. and J. Bennett (2008), 'Estimating intergenerational distribution preferences', *Ecological Economics*, **66**, 575–83.

Scarborough, H., M. Burton and J. Bennett (2009), 'Decision-making in a Social Welfare Context', Paper presented at Australian Agricultural Resource Economics Society Conference, http://purl.umn.edu/47672, accessed 12 April 2011.

Schwabe, K., P. Schuhmann, R. Boyd and K. Doroodian (2001), 'The value of changes in deer season length: an application of the nested multinomial logit model', *Environmental and Resource Economics*, **19** (2), 131–47.

Selten, R. and A. Ockenfels (1998), 'An experimental solidarity game', *Journal of Economic Behavior and Organisation*, **34** (4), 517–39.

Sen, A. (1974), 'Informational bases of alternative welfare approaches: aggregation and income distribution', *Journal of Public Economics*, **3** (4), 387–403.

Sen, A. (1977), 'On weights and measures', *Econometrica*, **45**, 1539–72.

Sen, A (1982), *Choice, Welfare and Measurement*, Oxford: Basil Blackwell.

Sen, A. (2000), 'Social Justice and the Distribution of Income', in A. Atkinson and F. Bourguignon (eds), *Handbook of Income Distribution*, Amsterdam: Elsevier Science, pp. 59–85.

Sen, A. (2009), *The Idea of Justice*, London: Allen Lane.

Serret, Y. and N. Johnstone (2006), *The Distributional Effects of Environmental Policy*, Cheltenham, UK and Northampton, MA, USA: Edward Elgar.

Shadish, W., T. Cook and D. Campbell (2002), *Experimental and Quasi-Experimental Designs for Generalized Causal Inference*, Boston: Houghton Mifflin.

Simon, H. (1956), 'Rational choice and the structure of the environment', *Psychological Review*, **63**, 129–38.

Solow, R. (1986), 'On the intergenerational allocation of natural resources', *The Scandinavian Journal of Economics*, **88** (1), 141–9.

Spash, C. (1994), 'Double CO_2 and beyond: benefits, costs and compensation', *Ecological Economics*, **10**, 27–36.

Squire, L. and H. van der Tak (1975), *Economic Analysis of Projects*, Baltimore: Johns Hopkins University Press.

Stavins, R., A. Wagner and G. Wagner (2002), 'Interpreting Sustainability in Economic Terms: Dynamic Efficiency Plus Intergenerational Equity', FEEM Working Paper No. 61.2002; and KSG Working Paper Series RWP 02-018, http://ssrn.com/abstract=326521, accessed 12 April 2011.

Stern, N. (2007), *The Economics of Climate Change: The Stern Review*, Cambridge: Cambridge University Press.

Sutherland, R. (2006), 'The Distributive Effects of Direct Regulation: A Case Study of Energy Efficiency Appliance Standards', in Y. Serret and N. Johnstone (eds), *The Distributional Effects of Environmental Policy*,

Cheltenham, UK and Northampton, MA, USA: Edward Elgar, pp.171–96.

Sumaila, U. and C. Walters (2005), 'Intergenerational discounting: a new intuitive approach', *Ecological Economics*, **52**, 135–42.

Svedsäter, H. (2003), 'Economic valuation of the environment: how citizens make sense of contingent valuation questions', *Land Economics*, **79** (1), 122–35.

Syme, G., B. Nancarrow and J. McCreddin (1999), 'Defining the components of fairness in the allocation of water to environmental and human uses', *Journal of Environmental Management*, **57**, 51–70.

Tabellini, G. (1991), 'The politics of intergenerational redistribution', *Journal of Political Economy*, **99**, 335–57.

Tacconi, L. (2000), *Biodiversity and Ecological Economics: Participatory Approaches to Resources Management*, London: Earthscan.

Tacconi, L. and J. Bennett (1995), 'Economic implications of intergenerational equity for biodiversity conservation', *Ecological Economics*, **12**, 209–23.

Thurstone, L. (1927), 'A law of comparative judgement', *Psychological Review*, **4**, 273–86.

Tietenberg, T. (2006), *Environmental and Natural Resource Economics*, 7th edition, Boston: Pearson.

Toman, M. (1994), 'Economics and sustainability: balancing trade-offs and imperatives', *Land Economics*, **70** (4), 399–413.

Train, K. (2003), *Discrete Choice Methods with Simulation*, Cambridge: Cambridge University Press.

Turner, R. (1988), 'Wetland conservation: economics and ethics', in D. Collard, D. Pearce and D. Ulph (eds), *Economics, Growth and Sustainable Environments*, London: Macmillan, pp. 121–59.

United Nations Conference on Environment and Development (UNCED) (1993), *Agenda 21: The United Nations Programme of Action from Rio*, New York: United Nations Dept. of Public Information.

Wang, X., J. Bennett, C. Xie, Z. Zhang and D. Liang (2006), 'Estimating non-market environmental benefits of the conversion of cropland to forest and grassland program: a choice modelling approach', *Ecological Economics*, **63** (1), 114–125.

Weisbrod, B. (1964), 'Collective-consumption services of individual-consumption goods', *Quarterly Journal of Economics*, **78** (3), 471–77.

Weisbrod, B. (1972), 'Deriving an Implicit Set of Governmental Weights for Income Classes', in R. Layard (ed.), *Cost–Benefit Analysis, Selected Readings*, Middlesex: Penguin Books, pp. 395–428.

Wills, I. (2006), *Economics and the Environment: A Signalling and Incentives Approach*, 2nd edition, Sydney: Allen & Unwin.

World Bank (1996), *Handbook on Economic Analysis and Investment Operations*, Washington, DC: World Bank.

World Commission on Environment and Development (1987), *Our Common Future: The Brundtland Report*, New York: Oxford University Press.

Yitzhaki, S. (2003), 'Cost–benefit analysis and the distributional consequences of government projects', *National Tax Journal*, **LV1** (2), 319–36.

Index